THE ART OF

CROSSING CULTURES

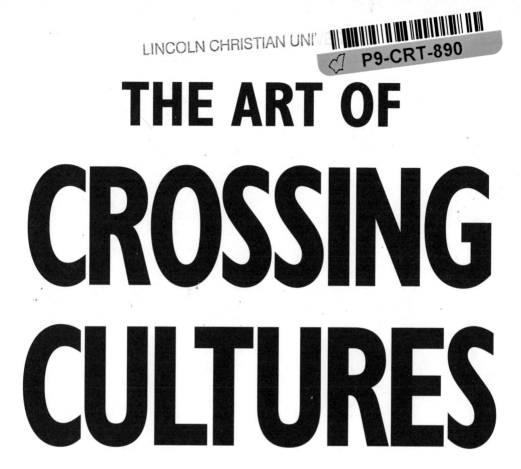

THE ART OF
CROSSING CULTURES

NICHOLAS BREALEY
PUBLISHING

BOSTON LONDON

First published by Nicholas Brealey Publishing in association with Intercultural Press in 2001. Reprinted in 2002, 2004, and 2006. This edition published by Intercultural Press in 2007.

Intercultural Press, Inc.
a division of Nicholas Brealey Publishing
20 Park Plaza, Suite 1115A
Boston, MA 02116 USA
Tel: 617-523-3801
Fax: 617-523-3708
www.interculturalpress.com

Nicholas Brealey Publishing
3–5 Spafield Street
London EC1R 4QB, UK
Tel: +44-207-239-0360
Fax: 44-207-239-0370
www.nicholasbrealey.com

Cover design: Ken Leeder

ISBN-13: 978-1-931930-53-6
ISBN-10: 1-931930-53-8

Printed in the United States

11 10 09 08 07   6 7 8 9 10

Library of Congress Cataloging-in-Publication Data
Storti, Craig.
   Art of crossing cultures/Craig Storti.—2nd ed.
      p. cm.
   Includes bibliographical references and index.
   ISBN 1-85788-296-2
      1. Culture shock. 2. Intercultural communication. 3. Assimilation
(Sociology) I. Title.
      GN517.S76 2001
      303.48′2—dc21   2001024373

Substantial discounts on bulk quantities are available. For details, discount information, or to request a free catalogue, please contact the publishers at the addresses given above.

Dedication

To my Teachers,
Mother Sayamagyi and
Sayagyi U Chit Tin,
with deepest respects
and gratitude

Table of Contents

Preface to the Second Edition

Authors are never completely finished with their books. They may turn in their manuscripts on the agreed-upon day, but deep down they know if they only had more time, they could say it better. Revised editions call an author's bluff; if you really could have said it better, here's your chance.

Readers will have to judge whether the first or this second edition of *The Art of Crossing Cultures* says it better, but this new edition does say some things differently—and some new things altogether. The conceptual framework of the original is still here, as is the model of cultural adjustment, now called "cultural effectiveness," though the model itself has been modified in important respects. There are now 7 chapters instead of 9; chapters 5 and 6 have been combined, and the last chapter, on repatriation, has been dropped, having been superseded by this author's own *The Art of Coming Home* (also being issued in a revised edition) and because it did not seem to fit with this edition's more singular focus on the overseas experience.

Other changes include a considerably expanded first chapter on country shock, the use of more illustrations from the world of business, and the addition of a new appendix ("Eloquent Witness") of quotations on the overseas experience. Finally, the chapter titles have become decidedly more prosaic. While "The Howling of Tigers, The Hissing of Serpents" (old title) is certainly more evocative than "Country Shock" (new title), it is not nearly as descriptive, as chapter titles have some obligation to be. Make no mistake; tigers still howl and serpents still hiss in these pages, but no longer in chapter titles.

—Craig Storti
Westminster, Maryland
June 2001

Foreword to the First Edition

Once every decade in every discipline of study, a book comes along which does more than inform and entertain. It enlightens. I have a hunch that *The Art of Crossing Cultures* will be such a book for the intercultural field.

The interesting thing about *The Art of Crossing Cultures* is that it will be as enlightening to the university student in a formal intercultural communication course as it will be to the practical-minded businessperson bound for a first overseas assignment and as it will be for the seasoned intercultural specialist who is forever looking for theoretical material to explain the process we have all experienced but have such difficulty putting into words.

The selected quotations from literary sources are themselves worth the price of the book. They are truly delightful, making their points with clarity and charm, and adding their own additional insights to those of Craig Storti.

It is a pleasure to discover such a literate new writer contributing to our field and to share, even for a moment, this paper podium with him.

—L. Robert Kohls
San Francisco, February 1989

Acknowledgments

It has been twelve years since David Hoopes received a manuscript out of the blue one day from a guy no one had ever heard of. He not only read it, kindness enough, he published it. Now, there's a risk taker. I shall always be deeply grateful. Then Bob Kohls weighed in—a guy everyone has heard of—with his generous foreword. And all the while Sandy Fowler and Fanchon Silberstein were uncommonly supportive.

In Maine Judy Carl-Hendrick worked her usual editing wonders on the first edition and has returned for a repeat performance, with none of her powers diminished. In London Nicholas Brealey was good enough to see trade potential in this book and wise enough to request a couple of important changes.

Toby Frank gets her own paragraph. She's the kind of publisher every writer dreams of: she listens to you rant and rave, heaps praise on your matchless prose (and then quietly edits it into even greater matchlessness), and generally confirms your belief that the universe does indeed revolve around you.

Pity the writer's wife. She has a front row seat at every crisis of confidence, every occasion when the words and thoughts don't come anymore, every time things don't go well. It can be tough writing a book, but it's nothing compared to living with a guy who's writing a book. To C., as always, my deepest thanks.

Introduction

*Now it is not good for the Christian's health to hustle the
Aryan brown*
*For the Christian riles and the Aryan smiles and he weareth
the Christian down.*
*And the end of the fight is a tombstone white with the name
of the late deceased,*
*And the epitaph drear: "A fool lies here who tried to hustle
the East."*

—Rudyard Kipling

If there's one thing nearly everyone who lives and works abroad
has to get right, it is this: they must be able to get along with the
local people. In whatever capacity they go overseas—whether for
business, diplomacy, the military, as an exchange or study abroad
student, as a development worker or civil servant—and whatever
their goals and responsibilities, it is difficult to imagine how they
can succeed if they can't interact effectively with people from the
local culture. And yet a great many expatriates cannot. This book
will explain why and what to do about it.

In the era of globalization, an increasing number of companies
and organizations are sending expatriates into the field, including

numerous smaller companies that never previously saw the need. In a 1999 survey of 264 U.S.-based multinational corporations, more than half of the respondents (52 percent) indicated they had increased their number of expatriate employees in the preceding year, and two-thirds said they expected their numbers to increase again by the year 2000 (Windham 1999, 8). With an ever-increasing number of companies earning more revenue from overseas than from domestic operations, first-hand knowledge and experience of foreign markets and conditions has become essential for today's managers and executives. For that same reason, the career path to senior management positions in most global companies now includes at least one overseas assignment. These assignments used to be for the adventurous and the nonconformists; now they're *de rigueur* for almost anyone who aspires to a leadership role in a company with foreign operations.

The Windham International survey cited above also identified the three leading causes of "assignment failure": partner dissatisfaction, family concerns, and the inability to adapt. All three causes, and especially the inability to adapt, suggest that successfully crossing cultures is a major challenge for most expatriates. "If left to luck," Robert Kohls has observed, "your chances of having a really satisfying experience living abroad would be about one in seven" (2001, 1).

The costs of cross-cultural failure, for individuals and their organizations, have been well documented. There are personal costs and family costs; financial, professional, and emotional costs; and costs to one's career prospects, to one's self-esteem, and to one's marriage and family. (Sixty-nine percent of the expats in the Windham study were married, and 61 percent were accompanied overseas by their children.) The organization may pay a steep price as well—in recruitment and selection costs, in training costs, moving costs, compromised careers, and all the costs associated with lost opportunities, damaged relationships, low morale, reduced productivity, and perhaps even damage to the company or organization's reputation in the country or region.

Nor are the costs of a failed assignment borne entirely by the individual expat and his or her parent company or organization. Most expats occupy high profile, senior positions, where the decisions they make directly or indirectly affect the lives of large numbers of people. They may start projects, initiate reforms, begin overhauls of various procedures or systems—and then bail out and leave the local people dangling. Local people often make job or career changes, which affect their whole family, based on initiatives or changes begun by the new head of this or chief of that—who then departs abruptly for home. The comings and goings of expats touch many local lives, in ways often not appreciated by those who are not around when the dust settles.

There are two typical endgames for expatriates who fail to effectively cross cultures: either they go home early from their overseas assignment, or, more commonly, they stay on, with greatly diminished effectiveness, often doing themselves, their families, and their organizations irreparable harm. Either way, it's an outcome no one desires.

This book explains why crossing cultures can be so difficult and how to minimize that difficulty and all the unfortunate consequences it leads to. After an opening chapter on country shock, the rest of the book takes the reader step by step through the process of encountering and learning to deal effectively with another culture, showing where most expats go wrong and how to keep that from happening.

This book is written primarily for expats themselves, who need to understand the experience they're going through, but it will also be useful to people from the local culture who work *with* expatriates. Anyone working alongside, supervising, or working under an expat is bound to benefit from understanding what it's like for that person to live and work in that country. The people back home who support and manage expats can also do their jobs better if they understand what an expat goes through overseas.

But enough prologue. Your plane has landed and even now is taxiing to the gate. In a few minutes, you'll be clearing customs and stepping out into a whole new world.

Take a deep breath. You're about to become a foreigner.

1

Country Shock

I have already mentioned the prickly heat, ringworm, dry gripes, putrid fevers, biles, consaca, and bloody flux, to which human nature is exposed in this Climate; also the mosquitoes, Patat and Scrapat lice, chigoes, cockroaches, ants, horse-flies, wild bees and bats, besides the thorns and briars, and the alligators and peree in the rivers; to which if we add the howling of tigers, the hissing of serpents, and the growling of Four—geoud, the dry, sandy savannahs, unfordable marshes, burning hot days, cold and damp nights, heavy rains, and short allowance, the reader may be astonished how any person was able to survive the trial. Notwithstanding this black catalogue, I solemnly declare I have omitted many other calamities that we suffered, as I wish to avoid [exaggeration].

—Captain John Stedman
Journey through Surinam

All in all, [this] is a really nice place to live and work. The people are friendly, the beaches are great, and the fried ants are delicious.

—Foreign aid worker,
East Africa

Before you can learn how to get along with the locals, you first have to survive the move abroad. While our focus in this book is on how to interact effectively with people from other cultures, this is not the only or even the first adjustment you have to make when you go overseas. You also have to get used to the new country—the new physical environment—to the new community, and to a new job (or, in the case of many expat spouses, to not having a job). Strictly speaking, these are not cultural adjustments (coming to terms with the behavior of the host country people), but they are very much part of the overall context in which cultural adjustment takes place. Occurring at the same time as cultural adjustment and competing for your attention and energy (neither of which is unlimited), these other adjustments inevitably affect the pace, and in many cases the outcome, of your struggle to adjust to the local culture. The impact of these other challenges is so direct and immediate that if you don't acknowledge and address the problems they pose early on, the resulting stress and anxiety can overwhelm and defeat you before you ever really encounter the culture. In short, while dealing effectively with what we might call these lesser adjustments may not constitute cultural adjustment, it could determine whether you ever get a chance to adjust to the people.

Some good news about these adjustments is that, unlike cultural adjustment, most of us have gone through them before. The typical expatriate has moved, for example, and has some idea of what's involved in adjusting to a new physical environment and to a new community, and most people have also changed jobs before and are familiar with the adjustments that involves. You might never before have done all of these at once—you can change jobs, for example, without moving—and you have probably not done them in an alien land, but at least you have some idea of what to expect and some of the skills you will need to cope.

A New Country

Climate

The first adjustments you make are to the new country, starting, unavoidably, with the climate. Whether you come from a dry climate and are set down in a humid one or from a cold climate and are set down in a warm one, you're going to notice the weather. We tend to think of climate or weather more as part of the scenery of an overseas experience, as a characteristic of the setting in which adjustment takes place, than as something else we have to adjust to. But climate can in fact wreak havoc on the unsuspecting expat: on your body, your health, your lifestyle, your pocketbook, and (sooner or later) your mind.

If you're not used to it, the heat and humidity of the tropics can be debilitating, even demoralizing. "I've been in Ceylon a month," D. H. Lawrence wrote on a visit to that country, "and nearly sweated myself into a shadow" (1984, 25). For the first few weeks, even months, you may feel a marked loss of energy, a need for more sleep, and any number of symptoms commonly associated with dehydration, such as headaches and low-grade fevers. You may have to rely on round-the-clock air-conditioning, though you consider it unhealthy; you may have to scrap plans to walk or bicycle to work (thus leaving your spouse at home without a car); you may have to give up tennis or jogging on your lunch hour, then gain weight because you don't get enough exercise; or you may have to buy new clothes, an unexpected expense; or your skin may break out, causing you to become depressed about your appearance. "The humidity could be blamed for many things," Anthony Burgess writes in *The Long Day Wanes*, "the need for a siesta, corpulence, the use of the car for a hundred-yard journey, the mildew on the shoes, the sweatrot in the armpits of dresses, the lost bridge-rubber or tennis-set, the dislike felt for the whole country" (1964, 36).

Nor is too cold much of an improvement on too hot. Older flats and homes in many countries don't come with central heating, for example, or they may have inadequate insulation. You can heat a room or two, perhaps (when the power is on), but you can't heat the entire house. You may bathe less frequently because it's too cold, and you may catch cold more easily.

Then, there's too wet—in the form of the monsoon that occurs each year throughout much of Asia and the Pacific: two to three months of relentless rain, flooded, impassable streets and roads, mold sprouting on your shoes and clothes and creeping down the walls. At least in the hot weather you can still go outside and move about, but in the monsoon you have no desire to do so (though you don't want to be inside either). Like excessive heat and cold, the monsoon not only makes you uncomfortable; it can make you unhappy.

4

Doing Without

Wherever you live overseas, the list of things "they don't have here" sometimes seems to have been designed with you personally in mind. Bad enough in itself, this list normally calls into being a second list—of the things you can't *do* here—and taken together these lists can make you very unhappy and frustrated. The lists are different in different places and for different expats; it may be a favorite food, a spice you can't cook without, replacement parts, a certain type of service, books in your native language, an appliance you can't live without, or a favorite sport or pastime. Learning to get by without these requires you to make scores of tiny adjustments every day, and while most people manage to cope well enough—finding substitutes or getting cherished items from loved ones back home—the annoyance and inconvenience of doing without take their toll. Any veteran expat will tell you that it's not just the big things that get to you overseas, like not speaking the language or understanding the locals, but also the count-less petty irritations that slowly wear you down. One famous story in the lore of expatriate failure tells of the man who came home early from his assignment in the South Pacific because, as he put it, "The salt wouldn't come out of the shaker."

The Loss of Routines

In a way, doing without is part of another, more all-encompassing issue, which we might call the loss of routines. Some observers claim that this is really the essence of adjusting to a new country, but whether it's the essence or not, it certainly looms large. But what are routines, and why is losing them such a problem? As this writer has noted elsewhere:

> *[A] routine is something you do while your mind is on something else, an action you have done so many times you no longer need to think about it in order to perform it. Most routines involve simple, uncomplicated behaviors that are easily mastered and that are always executed in a predict-able, unchanging manner. For most people, brushing their teeth is a routine, or, more accurately, many aspects of brush-ing one's teeth are routine. You don't have to be consciously aware of picking up your toothbrush, of opening the tube of toothpaste, of squeezing the tube, of raising your brush to your mouth, etc. You may give parts of this procedure fleet-ing attention, but you are probably giving conscious atten-tion to something else for most of the time it takes to brush your teeth. And the same can be said for numerous other actions and parts of actions you perform day in and day out.*
>
> *Many routines, though not all, involve basic coping and survival behaviors, such as bathing, dressing, eating, going to the bathroom, driving. More complicated behaviors can also become routines over time; for some people, cooking*

certain meals can be a routine. And even some of the most complicated behaviors can have routine elements. Routines by their very nature use up very little of your mental and physical energy, which is therefore available for higher order, more complicated—or brand new behaviors, which do require your mental and physical energy (at least until such time as they too are reduced, or reduced in part, to routines).

The lifeblood of routines is the known and the familiar. Needless to say, when you move to a new country, where nothing is known and familiar, your routines get mightily disrupted. Suddenly, nothing...is a routine. The loss of routines means the time and energy that were available for higher order, more sophisticated tasks now goes to basic coping and survival functions. With the minutiae of everyday life now demanding much of your conscious attention, [these higher order functions] either get put aside or take much longer to accomplish.... Many routines can be easily reestablished—the second time you brush your teeth overseas, the action is fast becoming automatic—but others can take longer to reconstruct.

The loss of routines hits you at your core. You expect to have to learn how to do new things overseas and even new ways of doing familiar things, but you may be surprised to discover that you have to learn to do things you normally do without thinking. (Storti 1997, 12–13)

Here's an expat describing the excitement of reestablishing a common routine, driving, his first day in England:

My very first day in England I went into work just to get the [company] car. It was a stick shift. I drove a stick shift about fifteen years ago for about a month.... The manager who was leaving drove me to a petrol station, filled it up for me and said, "Okay, here is your driving lesson." So I jerked

back to the office about a mile or two away and he pro-
ceeded to show me where all of the little gizmos were on the
car. He said, "Okay, you are on your own." And there I was
with the car and no map and two hundred miles to drive
that day with a stick shift, sitting on the wrong side of the
front seat. It was a little terrifying.... (Osland 1995, 38–39)

The problem with routines is that until you've reestablished them, you can have a very low opinion of yourself. If something this simple can be so difficult, then what am I going to do about something that's *genuinely* difficult?

Unfamiliar Faces

Another reality of being in a new country is not knowing anyone. For the first few weeks after your arrival, you will be interacting day in and day out, hour by hour, with people you don't know or don't know very well. There's nothing bad about this, of course—part of the adventure of being an expatriate is meeting new people—but it takes much more energy and effort than interacting with people you already know and who know you. When you are with people like this, you can relax and be yourself. Because you know they know you, you don't have to be especially careful of what you do and say to make sure they form a positive impression. With new people, however, who don't yet have an impression of you, you tend to be very careful of what you say and do until you see how they respond. Being careful like this, paying close, conscious attention to everything you say and do, takes considerable emotional and physical effort. A few hours of interacting with relative strangers, whether from your own or the host country, will leave you as tired as a whole day of dealing with people you already know.

A related problem is being so far away from family and friends. There's the homesickness dimension, genuinely missing close friends and loved ones, and there's also the matter of not having the support and encouragement such people offer us during difficult times. As you face the difficulties of those early months abroad, you need the kind of unconditional acceptance and support only close friends and family members can provide; you need people who will listen to your tirades about the country and the natives without judging, people with whom you can fall apart without being embarrassed or worrying about what they might think. Your spouse may be available for this purpose, of course, but he or she may be looking to you for the same support. Whenever possible, you should plan to fall apart on different days from your spouse.

Additional Issues in Developing Countries

Expatriates working in developing nations often face an extra set of "country" issues, those that their counterparts in more modern countries don't normally experience. The communications infrastructure, for example, is delicate in many developing countries, posing all manner of special problems in a world increasingly dependent on technology. The issue is not so much having the technology as it is having a reliable source of electricity. Electricity supply has always been a problem in the third-world, but it mattered less in a less-wired world. When the power goes out these days, as it does increasingly in many developing countries, the impact is much greater. Work stops, in a word, and out come the teacups.

Another chronic complaint is poor telephone service. While the situation has improved somewhat in the era of cell phones and satellite communications, any expat from a modern country who lives and works in a developing country has to adjust to considerably less reliable and efficient telephone service. Imagine for a moment having to actually visit, or send someone else to visit, a quarter or even a third of the local destinations you telephone or e-mail on an average day from work or from home. (And while you're at it, imagine not being able to contact at all some of the more far-flung destinations.) Without good telephone service, the amount of business you can conduct in Lahore or Harare may be only half what you are used to—and the effort may be double. In the West the telephone is like a third hand; when suddenly it's amputated, you miss it.

The absence of reliable communications is at least part of the reason for the expatriate's favorite complaint about how long it takes to get things done in developing countries. It likewise goes a long way toward explaining that other old standby about the slower pace of life in Asia or Latin America or around the shores of the Mediterranean. People have more time for each other, we hear; they enjoy each other's company more. While personal relationships are certainly more important in many countries than in the West, the fact is that when you can't call, you have to go, and a visit is naturally more personal than a telephone call and always takes longer. No one thinks it odd if you hang up after three minutes, but if you leave someone's home or office three minutes after arriving (when you spent half an hour just to get there) you would certainly be thought odd, or worse.

Transportation is another issue in many developing countries. If you can't call and the matter can't wait, then you have to go. Whether the problem is crumbling roads and bridges, old and unreliable equipment (stop lights, airplanes, repair and emergency vehicles), fuel shortages, or missing parts, a weak transportation infrastructure can make getting around the country expensive, extremely time-consuming, and, in many cases, downright dangerous. It is seventy-five miles from Colombo to Galle in Sri Lanka. If you leave at 8:30 A.M. for a 10 A.M. appointment, you'll be two hours late. If you need a spare part in Pokhara (Nepal) and it has to come from Khatmandu, ninety miles away, you can take off the rest of the week.

"It was not like other bad roads," Peter Fleming writes of a famous track he came across in Brazil,

> *which incommode you with continuous and petty malice. "Look how far we can go," they seem to say, as you crawl painfully along them, "and still be called a road." You hate them the more bitterly for the knowledge that they will keep certain bounds. They will madden you with minor obstacles, but in the end they will let you through.*
>
> *But with the road to Leopoldina it was not like this. It had no quarrel with us. It took no count of us at all. It did not fight a sly, delaying action, raising our hopes only to dash them, but always keeping them alive. It did not set out to tantalize us or gall us. It seemed, rather, preoccupied with its own troubles. It had never wished to be a road, and now it cursed itself for not refusing its function before it was too late. It lashed itself into a fury of self-reproach. It writhed in anguish. It was clearly a tormented thing. At any moment, we felt, it might decide to End it All.* (1985, 126)

Tiresome as the above frustrations can be, surely the most inconvenient and unnerving problem expatriates often face in developing countries is the near constant threat of getting sick. No other difficulty can be quite so unsettling or require more time and effort to circumvent. You might reasonably assume that expatriate party talk in Jakarta or Casablanca would revolve around issues of moment, such as the declining *rupiyah* or forecasts of another year of drought, but it touches just as often on the solidity of one's stools and how long to soak the lettuce in disinfectant. This is only natural: while you can learn to manage without a working telephone or central heating, you can't do anything if you're confined to bed. And the combination of the unhygienic conditions common in developing countries and the pristine vulnerability of the expatriate from the antiseptic, sterilized West virtually guarantees that, feverish and cramp-ridden, it is to bed you will retire more than once during those early months abroad. A related worry, of course, is the often substandard quality of local medical care.

The worst part about being sick abroad is not what it does to the body, but what it does to the mind. In most cases expatriates manage to cope with the physical discomfort, but they struggle with the emotional and psychological effects of getting sick overseas. Being immobilized by giardia or amoebiasis only heightens your already elevated sense of vulnerability and helplessness, your feeling of not being in control. You become depressed. Your resolve weakens. Doubt arises. Novelist Paul Scott writes of a character newly arrived in India: "Through most of his experience of the rains, he was chronically and depressingly off colour. Whatever he ate turned his bowels to water. In such circumstances a human being goes short on courage" (1979, 245). If I hadn't come here, you can't help feeling, none of this would have happened.

Have we mentioned insects yet? An annoyance barely noticed in more developed countries, insects can be the bane of your existence in many parts of the world. Ants, mosquitoes, chiggers, cockroaches, flies, gnats, mites, leeches, spiders, bedbugs—they come in nature's own bounty. They get into your food, your bed, your shoes, and your clothes. They find their way into your hair, your ears, your nose, and your mouth. They can make your skin itch, burn, sting, swell, or break out. They can keep you awake at night, make you sweat, give you a fever and the runs, or make you throw up. They can make you very unhappy.

Mary Kingsley, that intrepid Victorian traveler, had them pegged. "I should say," she wrote,

> looking back calmly upon the matter, that seventy-five percent of West African insects sting, five percent bite, and the rest are either prematurely or temporarily parasitic on the

*human race. And undoubtedly one of the worst things you
can do in West Africa is to take any notice of an insect. If you
see a thing that looks like a cross between a flying lobster and
a figure of Abraxes on a Gnostic gem, do not pay it the least
attention, never mind where it is; just keep quiet and hope it
will go away—for that's your best chance; you have none in a
stand-up fight with a good, thorough-going African insect.*
(1984, 205)

It may sound a bit extreme, but many expats will find Joyce Osland's
account of her early days in Burkino Faso not particularly far-
fetched. She writes,

*It was a small cement-block house with no ventilation, on
top of a laterite hill.... Since we were worried the baby might
get malaria from the numerous mosquitoes, we quickly put
up screens on the windows and doors, prompting our French
neighbors to ask, with flawless logic, "How will the flies get
out?" With some difficulty we even screened the vent pipes
that...let hot air escape from the false ceiling. Even so, the
inside walls of the house were too hot to touch during the
dry season. The town had electricity only from 6:00 to 10:00
P.M. and when the house went dark we discovered why no
one else had ever screened the vent pipes.... [T]he bats who
lived in the false ceiling used the vent pipes as their nightly
exit [and] came down into the house, looking for a way to
get outside. They swooshed through our humble home....
Nothing in Doctor Spock had prepared me for flying rodents
and I was terrified a bat would bite the baby if she rolled
against her mosquito net.... By the time our belongings arrived six months later, we had a batless house. We managed
to liberate our crate of household effects from customs just
before the customs building burned down. As I stood on our
porch gazing fondly at the long awaited crate, I noticed a
black tide moving toward the door...the crate was full of*

thousands of black ants, intent on taking over the house. I emitted a ladylike shriek and ran to put the baby in a safe place.... A passing African grabbed the hose and together we repulsed the invaders. (40–41)

A New Community

Another set of adjustments expatriates must make is to their new community. The challenge here is not so much emotional or psychological—as it is in adjusting to the new country—but practical. The issue is ignorance, not knowing anything about the community, and the solution is quite straightforward: learn about it. The only problem is that there's *so much* to learn.

One of the first things you have to learn about the community is how to find your way around—how it is laid out and where things are in relation to other things. The first time you drive to work or to the children's school or to the shopping district, you'll be quite disoriented. Not recognizing anything, you can't tell exactly where you are. Do I turn left or right at that church? Is that the same church I went by yesterday? This is normal in a new city, but it means you'll spend a lot longer just getting from place to place. If you don't speak the local language, finding your way around town is even more daunting, for you will be reluctant to ask people and thereby trigger one of those excruciating exchanges wherein the local citizen is trying hard to be helpful and you don't understand a word he or she is saying.

If you live in a large city, you may have to figure out how the subway or bus system works. Which train do I want? How do I know if it stops at my stop? How many of these little tokens do I need? Do I get on at the front of the bus or in the middle? How do I pay? What are these coins worth in the local currency? How do I know where to get off? Why is everyone staring at me?

Once you know where things are and how to get there, you have to understand how they work. What are the hours of these places? What's the "system" in a pharmacy, bank, post office, cinema, petrol station, market? How do the public telephones work? Will there be an attendant in the public lavatory whom I need to tip? Do I sit down and wait for someone to come to my table (in a bakery) or do I order at the counter?

Driving and parking can be especially nerve-wracking the first few times you go out. What do the curb markings and sidewalk signs say? What do the lane markings mean? Is this a one-way street? Can I turn left here? What's the speed limit? Is this the day cars with my kind of license plate are allowed in the city center? Where are the parking lots and garages and how do I pay? Is that an entrance or an exit? Why is that guy honking at me?

The first two or three weeks overseas are full of these kinds of incidents, situations where you don't know quite what you're supposed to do but know you have to do something. You can laugh them off to a point—they're all quite petty in the grand scheme of things—but most people tire quite quickly of making fools of themselves. These incidents may make for good stories later, but they're no fun when they're happening. One saving grace is that these kinds of problems aren't difficult to solve; your second subway ride or visit to the bank goes more smoothly than the first. On the other hand, the sheer number of such incidents can quickly become overwhelming. If you weren't going through scores of other adjustments at the same time, these minor irritations might not matter so much, but you are, so minor annoyances sometimes feel like catastrophies.

A New Job

Finally, there is adjusting to your new job. Apart from the cultural differences (which we take up in the next chapter), any new job poses challenges. The biggest may be getting used to the change from being at the top of your form one moment, during your final months in your previous position, to being all thumbs the next. When you change jobs, after all, you leave a familiar situation, where you were very good at what you were doing, to go to a wholly unfamiliar situation, where you will initially be inept and incompetent. It's disconcerting in the best of circumstances to come face to face with your inadequacies, but it's especially hard when you are in the habit of excelling.

A new job often means new responsibilities and new skills to master, which will take time and effort. There will also be numerous procedures, regulations, and office protocols to learn, and many of your work routines will have to be painstakingly reestablished. As a result, you will have to be satisfied, in the near future, with smaller achievements than you may be used to. While you will one day be able to triumph, your goal for the moment must be to cope.

A new job may also mean all new colleagues, an office or division full of people you've never worked with before. People will be taking your measure even as you take theirs. You will have to spend several weeks carefully observing your colleagues and trying to take your cues from them, monitoring everything you do and say so as to make a favorable impression. Maintaining this high degree of self-awareness takes considerable effort and energy, neither of which the typical expat has in abundance.

Issues for Spouses

Several studies have found that the most common reason expat employees fail to function effectively on an overseas assignment is the inability of the spouse to adjust to the new environment. This is not because spouses aren't as good at adjusting as the working partner; it's because spouses, it turns out, have much more to adjust *to*. They face all the adjustments already mentioned (except to a new job) and a number of others unique to their situation.

Let's start with work. While some spouses find work overseas, the majority do not (Black, Gregersen, and Mendenhall 1992, 130). For those who are used to working, and especially for those with well-established careers, being unable to work can wreak havoc on their personal and professional identity. Spouses who defined themselves by and took satisfaction in their work back home may now feel unsure of themselves and unfulfilled. They may very well fashion a new identity for themselves, but it can be a slow and difficult process.

Meanwhile, these spouses have to figure out how to fill up a day having little or no structure. As nice as it can be to have some time to oneself, eight hours a day is more than most people bargain for. "[I was always] trying to find things to do with my time," one spouse remembers. "I spent time sewing, and I *hate* to sew" (Adler 1986, 232). In many countries the situation is made worse by the custom of having household help; spouses who might have been inclined to fill their day looking after the house, taking care of small children, and preparing meals don't have even those outlets. "I felt useless," another spouse recalls. "I was a fifth wheel" (232). Spouses sick of household chores, on the other hand, won't find this feature of overseas life hard to get used to.

Loneliness typically strikes the at-home spouse harder than it does the employee, especially if the at-home spouse worked before going overseas. The employed spouse, after all, is surrounded all day by colleagues and co-workers, but if the at-home spouse wants to interact with people, he or she has to make it happen. "I was very lonely," one spouse remembers, "and my husband was not going through the same problems I [was]. And I felt more lonely because I couldn't share my problems with him" (231).

The at-home spouse also gets a bigger dose of culture shock

than the typical employee. In many cases the working spouse spends the day in an environment very reminiscent of the work environment back home. Co-workers may either be compatriots or locals who speak their home country language, and the activities and rhythm of the workday are often very familiar. Even when he or she ventures out of the workplace, it's usually to go to another, very similar workplace to interact with people more like oneself. But the at-home spouse lives very much in the local culture, if not inside the home itself (and there too, if there are servants), then every time someone comes to the door (the repairman, the flower seller) and every time the spouse goes out. Not surprisingly, expat spouses typically learn the local language faster than working spouses.

"I had the fort of the office," one working spouse remembers.

> *And very often I would work seven days a week, just because it was comfortable. I had my desk and my stapler; and the people there...knew who I was and would take care of me...and it took a while to get out onto the street. It was a strain on the family because I left it all to them. I left the problems to them while I went to work.* (Osland, 43)

The at-home spouse also has a ringside seat from which to watch the adjustment of the children. While working spouses are also involved in the children's adjustment, they're often not as close to the drama as the primary caregiver. This is especially true when the working spouse is on the road a great deal, which is often the case with expat assignments.

Finally, many expat spouses have to come to terms with what is often called the resentment issue. When all is said and done, expat families usually go overseas because of an opportunity that became available for either the husband or the wife, but only rarely for both. While it's almost always a mutual decision, made after carefully weighing all the pros and cons for all family members, one spouse is almost always less enthusiastic than the other and likewise has to give up more than the other. For reasons just explained, at-home spouses typically make the greater sacrifice and also face more—and more difficult—adjustments than do employees. It is not surprising, then, that spouses typically have more occasion to regret the decision to move abroad, which often leads to feelings of resentment toward their partners. And then—and this is the core of the resentment issue—they feel bad for blaming their partner for what was, after all, a joint decision. It's really nobody's fault, and yet....

Not all spouses will have all of these issues, nor is the life of an expat spouse merely one problem after another. It can also be a very liberating, enriching, and otherwise satisfying experience. But spouses would be wise to be prepared for the good times *and* the bad.

Consequences

What does it mean to be faced with all these adjustments? If you could deal with them one at a time, they wouldn't pose such a problem, but they don't appear one at a time, each patiently waiting its turn; they tend, rather, to travel in packs, ganging up on you at inopportune moments. Or if they weren't so numerous, they might also be manageable; it's not the nature of these adjustments that makes them so daunting, but the sheer number and variety.

One thing it means is that you're going to be tired and under the weather a lot during your early weeks abroad. Individually and collectively, these adjustments demand a great deal of mental exertion, which can leave you physically and emotionally drained. And that, in turn, leaves you an easy mark for all manner of low-grade infections, fevers, and colds. Cornelius Grove has explained that clinically speaking *the reason why intercultural contact—especially a complete immersion experience—potentially results in this condition is that the sojourner is obliged to respond not merely to isolated instances of novelty in an otherwise familiar and reasonably predictable environment, but to novelties throughout many or most of the subtle and complex patterns of daily life.... Usually the problem is not that a single stressor in the new environment is completely overwhelming, but rather that the body must respond to multiple stressors on a constant basis over a period of time lasting throughout the first several weeks or even months of the sojourn....*

Stress [becomes] a problem when the neurological and endocrine systems are compelled to respond to environmental novelty constantly over a long period of time. When this happens, the neurological system, and especially the endocrine system, can become debilitated through overstimulation. [Among the] consequences [are] a sharp reduction in the production of white blood cells...which in turn leads to susceptibility to various diseases and/or exacerbation of chronic illness. Furthermore, the body becomes more and more exhausted as energy is used constantly...to keep the brain and sensory organs in a high state of alertness, and to keep the body ready for fight, flight, or adaptation.

Physiologically speaking, culture shock is precisely this state of debilitation, exhaustion, and susceptibility to disease. (Grove 1990, 9)

Some other consequences of adjusting to so much that is new and different are frustration, anger, irritability, and impatience. And from time to time you may also feel threatened, vulnerable, anxious, incompetent, and foolish. Your self-esteem and self-confidence, in short, take quite a beating.

What Can You Do?

You don't have to take all this lying down (unless you're sick in bed); there are things you can do about culture shock. The first and most important is to know it's coming; part of the shock of country shock is not expecting it, which causes you to react more strongly when you encounter it. Knowing these experiences are coming doesn't mean you won't get sick or feel the heat, but awareness at least mutes the psychological/emotional impact. You'll still throw up, but you'll be much calmer about it.

You should also remember that many of these experiences aren't new. This isn't the first time you've adjusted to new people, a new community, new job responsibilities. All this chaos may be taking place in a very exotic location, but if you strip these adjustments down to their essence, there's not much here you haven't tangled with before. The scale of what you face may be novel—you may never have had to adjust to so much all at once—but the nature of what you're doing should be familiar. You can console yourself, then, with the knowledge that you already have most of the skills and instincts you need to prevail. You might have to apply them more deliberately and consciously, but you don't have to make them up on the spot.

Try to stay healthy and get plenty of rest. You can't avoid Captain Stedman's "black catalogue," the list of adjustments we've described, but you at least have control over what you eat and how much sleep you can get. Try also to do those things you normally do to unwind and relax, those things that rejuvenate you and lift your spirits.

Stay in touch with family and close friends back home. It's comforting to know that other people are concerned and care about you. Especially until you make good friends abroad, you need to stay connected to people who care about you back home.

Go out; see people; do things. If you're like most people, you may not feel like being around other people when you're depressed or off your stride. You're bad company, you think, and shouldn't inflict your low spirits on others, so you don't accept invitations or invite people over. But this only feeds your depression, whereas being with and having to respond to others makes you turn your attention away from your troubles for a bit. In the process, you're likely to discover that other people are having at least some of the same reactions to being overseas that you are.

Don't be too hard on yourself. We're not talking here about getting the hang of one or two new paradigms; it's a whole new world. And whole new worlds can take some getting used to. So you can be forgiven for feeling a tad overwhelmed, for wondering what you've gotten yourself into or whether you've done the right thing, and for being irritable and not much fun to be around. Expats sometimes worry that they must be going about this all wrong, that other people in their situation know something they don't or aren't having the same misgivings. "If only I had...." Relax; the problem isn't you.

Meanwhile, try to keep the big picture in mind. What if it is annoying running around Jakarta because the phones are out again, or learning to live without central heating or fresh oregano? Isn't this what you came for—for something different, the occasional adventure, a dash of risk and hardship? Surely you don't pull up your roots and take yourself and your family halfway around the world in the hope that everything will be exactly as it is back home. Where's the sense of accomplishment if there are no obstacles to surmount? How can you learn and grow from your experiences if you don't have any? "You have to be able to sustain reversals, upsets, accidents," Philip Glazebrook writes in *Journey to Kars*.

> *Things going wrong gives you the chance to show self-reliance; and isn't the assertion of self-reliance one of the chief*

objects of independent travel? If I'd really been separated from my [bags], a couple of days of dogged ingenuity would have been needed to reunite me with them, but it could have been done, and if I'd achieved it, I'd have felt extremely pleased with myself. (1984, 20)

Lord Byron would have agreed. He once ranked life's pursuits and concluded that gambling, battle, and travel were the foremost. Their "particular attraction," he noted, lay in "the agitation inseparable from their accomplishment. [They make us] feel that we exist" (Fussell 1987, 14).

● ● ●

This, then, is what we have called country shock. Yet for all its variety and abundance, country shock is not the main event in these pages. It will not have escaped the astute reader that we have yet to meet a single host country person in this chapter. Strictly speaking, nothing we've talked about thus far comes under the heading of culture—the attitudes, values, and behaviors of the local people and their response to yours. You can adjust to the country, in other words, and to the community, and even to the job, and still not be able to get along with the locals. And if you can't get along with the locals, you will never be successful in an overseas assignment.

It's important, then, not to confuse adjusting to the country with adjusting to the culture. You will begin to get used to, understand, and function effectively in more and more of the situations we've described in this chapter. In a matter of weeks, some things that were very trying will gradually become second nature, and some others that seemed impossible will look less daunting. You will begin to feel comfortable and competent in more situations: at home, on the job, out in the streets and shops. But you should not let this growing sense of well-being and self-confidence blind you to the true nature of your achievements. Simply because you've found the bakery or figured out the bus routes doesn't mean you understand the culture. Getting used to curry isn't the same as getting used to the people who eat curry.

Indeed, during the first few weeks of an overseas assignment, it's not unusual for expats to be somewhat insulated from many of the realities of life in the new country. People at work understand that you're new and a little overwhelmed, and other expats remember their first few weeks all too well and protect you from the rougher edges of the culture until you've toughened up. Your organization may run interference for you, handling many of the logistical details of settling in that might otherwise defeat you. In these and other ways, you're shielded from all but occasional contact with the local culture and could, therefore, be forgiven for thinking you've adjusted when in actual fact real contact, hence true adjustment, has yet to begin.

By all means, go ahead and pat yourself on the back as you score small triumphs, but stay alert. Country shock, for all its challenges and frustrations, is in many ways just a sideshow; the main event—adjusting to the culture—is about to begin.

2

Culture Shock

*What strikes me the most upon the whole is the total differ-
ence of manners between them and us, from the greatest
object to the least. There is not the smallest similitude in
the twenty-four hours. It is obvious in every trifle.*

—Horace Walpole
Letters

To succeed in an overseas assignment, expats have to interact effectively with the local people. Since most of those people are
foreigners, and since the expat is a foreigner to them, succeeding
abroad means being able to work effectively across cultures. And
there's the rub: because of cultural *differences*—different, deeply
held beliefs and instincts about what is natural, normal, right,
and good—*cross*-cultural interactions are subject to all manner of
confusion, misunderstanding, and misinterpretation. In a word,
they are often unsuccessful. Cross-cultural encounters don't always go wrong, of course, any more than same-culture interactions always go splendidly, but, all other things being equal, they
are certainly more *likely* to end badly. In the remainder of this
book, we will explain why this happens and offer guidelines for
how to prevent it.

Cultural "Incidents"

How do we define an unsuccessful interaction? For our purposes here, we will consider a cross-cultural encounter to have gone wrong whenever one or more of the parties is confused, offended, frustrated, or otherwise put off by the behavior of any of the other parties. In workplace terms, a cross-cultural interaction has gone wrong when it has in any substantial way undermined the ability or the desire of one or more of the parties to continue to work together. If the expatriate manager of overseas operations clashes repeatedly with a local, host country service provider, that relationship will be weakened and the service threatened. If the expat head of accounting doesn't get along with her team of local CPAs, that division's performance is going to suffer. If a negotiator thinks the other side is lying, common ground may be hard to find. If an expat spouse feels she is harassed by men at the local bakery cafe, she may turn against the culture.

By itself, no single cross-cultural "incident," as we will call these unsuccessful encounters, is going to sabotage an overseas sojourn or compromise a business or workplace relationship. But over time and in the aggregate, such incidents can slowly—and in some cases, quite rapidly—undermine relations between expats and the local people to the extent that constructive, successful interaction is no longer possible. Expats may very well continue in their assignments beyond this point, but they are no longer benefiting themselves or their organization; indeed, as we shall see in the next chapter, they may very well be causing serious harm to both. If expats, whether spouses or employees, are to have an effective and positive overseas experience, then, in the lexicon of this book, cross-cultural incidents must be kept to a minimum.

Before we consider why these incidents occur and how to prevent them, let's look at some examples. This book divides cross-cultural incidents into two types: *Type I* are those incidents where the behavior of someone from another culture confuses, frustrates, or otherwise puts expats off. *Type II* are those incidents where the expat's behavior confuses, frustrates, or otherwise puts off someone from another culture. In the first instance the expat is the "victim," if you will, of the annoying behavior, and in the second, the expat is the perpetrator. In both cases, incidentally, it is the expat who suffers the most.

This distinction is, in one sense, artificial, for in fact the same problem or phenomenon—one person offending another person—is occurring in each type of incident; the only thing that changes is the perspective. But this distinction is important. Expats need to realize that it's not just *their* reactions to the local culture (what we're calling a Type I incident) that can undermine a cross-cultural relationship, but also the reactions of local people to the expat's culture (a Type II incident). You could be in a cross-cultural partnership, for example, where you have no complaints about your partner (where there haven't been any Type I incidents). But your partner, although managing to keep you quite happy, may frequently be put off by your behavior and want to end the relationship. Culture is still getting in the way here, if only in one direction, and this partnership cannot be considered a success. By definition, relationships only work when both partners are comfortable. To be truly effective, cross-cultural partnerships must be relatively free of both Type I *and* Type II incidents.

Type I: Expats Reacting to the Behavior of People from the Local Culture

But we're getting ahead of ourselves. Let's look at examples of the two types of incidents to see what actually happens when people from different cultures meet. We begin with examples of Type I.

> *You're a European software engineer managing a team of Indian programmers in charge of developing and testing an*

important new application. You have an imminent deadline and have just explained to your team how to fix a new bug that has been detected. When you ask the team if they have understood your explanation, they say yes and return to their cubicles. The next day, when you check in with them, they have made no progress whatsoever, and it turns out they did not understand your explanation. You've lost twenty-four hours you can't afford to waste and are not happy.

You are the female expatriate manager of the Cairo-based operations of the British company you work for. The head of accounting, an Egyptian man, isn't used to working under a woman. On several occasions in the last month, he has double-checked instructions from you with your male deputy, another British expat, before obeying them. This is a nuisance for your deputy, and it's upsetting to you.

"I was once called in to advise [a multinational] firm that has operations all over the world," Edward Hall writes. "One of the first questions they asked was, 'How do you get Germans to keep their doors open?' Closed doors gave [my clients] the feeling that there was a conspiratorial air about the place and that they were being left out."

—Edward Hall
The Hidden Dimension

You're a professor teaching at one of the overseas campuses of the university you work for. When you give your first exam, you notice that some students are copying from the papers of other students, and others are referring to or copying information from papers they have brought to class. You are very upset at these instances of cheating.

You're the American in charge of your company's operations in Singapore. You have an extremely well-qualified deputy to whom you have delegated all responsibility for a number of important tasks. But he seems reluctant to make even the most routine decisions, insisting on checking with you before acting on any matter of importance. This is very time-consuming and frustrating for you.

"One of the terms most frequently used by Americans to describe the Japanese modus operandi," Hall has observed, *"is the word* indirection. *An American banker who had just spent years in Japan and made the minimum possible accommodation told me that what he found most frustrating and difficult was their indirection. 'An old-style Japanese,' he complained, 'can drive a man crazy faster than anything I know. They talk around and around and around a point and never do get to it.'"*

—Edward Hall
The Hidden Dimension

29

You're an expat spouse posted in France. You're walking down the street with a French friend one day when she meets a friend of hers, and they engage in conversation. You are surprised and hurt when the conversation ends and you have not been introduced to your friend's friend.

You have been negotiating with a Chinese service provider on behalf of your company. You and your counterpart have finally agreed on terms and signed a four-year contract. Three weeks later, after you have incurred considerable start-up costs, your Chinese counterpart telephones to inform you his department has come under new management and the contract has to be renegotiated. You remind him there were

*safeguards in the original contract against such contingen-
cies, but he says they cannot be enforced in his country.*

*You're an American expatriate working in Buenos Aires. You
have a 10:00 A.M. appointment with the Argentinian manager of a local public relations firm, and it's now 10:30. The
receptionist tells you the person you've come to see is meeting with someone else. You wait another half an hour, during which time another person (who has the next appointment?) arrives. You become increasingly frustrated until, at
11:00 A.M., the manager emerges from his office to greet
you. To your amazement, he neither acknowledges nor apologizes for making you wait an hour. You find this behavior
extremely rude and are furious with him.*

*You're an Argentinian expatriate working in the United States.
You're meeting with the American sales director of one your
company's local subsidiaries. Suddenly, at 10:30 A.M., she
announces that you and she will have to continue this meeting later, "maybe this afternoon or tomorrow morning,"
because she has another appointment at this time. You're
very surprised and upset not to be able to finish your business and to have to go to the trouble of coming back again
later.*

Not surprisingly, Type I incidents are the stock in trade of the best
travel writers, so we conclude our list with a few examples from
travel literature.

*Nothing is more charming than southern courtesy, but some-
times they really are too sympathetic by half. For in order
not to contradict you or give you a moment's pain by dis-
puting the accuracy of your ideas, they will tell you what
you want to hear rather than what would be of real use to*

you to hear. At the same time their own self-esteem will not permit them to confess a blank ignorance; they will rather tell you something incorrect than tell you nothing at all.

—Aldous Huxley
Along the Road

"I am not the type, monsieur, who feels himself superior to the rest of humanity. Indeed, I am no better than others. But these people, these Afghans. They are not human." "But why do you say that?" "You don't see why, monsieur? Have you eyes? Look at those men over there. Are they not eating with their hands? With their hands! It is frightful."

—Robert Byron
The Road to Oxiana

Indians do seem uncouth to the European. I shared the compartment with fat Mr. Jain, a vegetarian with swollen lips of the kind known as sensual, mouth and teeth red-stained from betel juice, who punctuated the dark hours with snores and farts and hawkings—all Indians appear to do this. Yesterday morning an American family was having breakfast with their guide who, in mid-conversation, gave vent to an elaborate hawking and clearing of the passages; they regarded their cornflakes expressionlessly.

—J. G. Farrell
Indian Diary

There is nothing so vile or repugnant to nature, but you may plead prescription for it in the customs of some nation or other. A Parisian likes mortified flesh; a native of Legiboli will not taste his fish until it is quite putrefied; the civilized inhabitants of Kamschatka get drunk with the urine of their guests, whom they have already intoxicated; the Nova

Zemblans make merry on train oil; the Greenlanders eat in
the same dish as their dogs; the Caffres, at the Cape of Good
Hope, piss upon those whom they delight to honor, and feast
upon a sheep's intestines with their contents as the greatest
dainty that can be presented.

—Tobias Smollett
Travels through France and Italy

These are a few of the ways people from other cultures can frustrate and put you off. In isolation, as noted earlier, these incidents have a limited impact, but when you live overseas, they don't occur in isolation. You are, after all, surrounded by foreigners (though you are the real foreigner), with whom any interaction has the potential of becoming a Type I incident (and, as we'll see shortly, a Type II incident as well). When your whole day is punctuated by these incidents, followed by another such day, and then another, the strain of crossing cultures begins to takes its toll. In a moment, we'll show you how by conjuring up a typical morning in the life of an expat, but first some examples of Type II incidents.

Type II: Local People Reacting to Expats

A cross-cultural encounter, by definition, is a two-way process. Even as you're being thrown by the annoying, unaccountable behaviors of the other person, chances are that person is also being put off by you. Let's look now at examples of Type II incidents.

You're an expat managing a team of software developers in
the Philippines. At a recent meeting, you've given the team
feedback on their work, beginning with a few remarks on
how pleased you are in general with the quality and speed
of their effort. You then spend a few more minutes mention-
ing two minor areas where things could be minimally im-
proved. You learn later that in the Philippines what you

have done constitutes damning with faint praise and is exactly how many Filipino managers would let a team know they were quite unhappy with its work. These managers, however, would never deliver this kind of feedback in a general meeting, thereby embarrassing the team leaders in front of their subordinates.

You're the New Delhi-based regional manager of your company's operations in the Middle East and South Asia. On a trip back to headquarters in Europe, you have a short stopover in Amman where you have scheduled a one-hour meeting with your Jordanian colleague who is in charge of marketing and public relations in the Middle East. Hussein wants to catch up on personal and family matters, but you feel pressured to resolve a couple of issues that have come up in the last several months, so you cut off the "small talk." You learn later that he was upset that you had only allowed an hour for this meeting and assumed this meant that you were angry with him about something. Moreover, when you then cut off the obligatory chitchat that always precedes business in the Middle East, he decided you must be on the verge of cancelling the contract with his company. In fact, he may now cancel the contract first, in a pre-emptive move to save face.

You're a newly arrived American expat couple living in London. On Friday the working spouse learned that one of his English colleagues lives in the same neighborhood as you, so he wrote down the English family's street name and house number. On Sunday afternoon, while you're out for a walk, you happen by the house and decide to drop in. You learn later that among middle- and upper-class English people it's considered extremely rude to drop by someone's house unannounced.

You're a visiting British professor in a South American university. You think the role of the teacher is to help students learn how to learn, to help them develop problem-solving skills. You teach through case studies and other problem-posing methods and ask lots of questions. To your surprise, you learn that the students in your class are upset and have complained to the department chair that you're not teaching them anything, not passing on your knowledge and wisdom.

You're the expat manager of your Dutch company's affiliate operations in Mexico City. At a weekly meeting of division heads (where each is accompanied by two or three support staff), you correct some inaccurate sales figures quoted by the director of Sales and Marketing. You learn later that to correct her like this in front of her subordinates makes her look very bad and makes you look unkind and insensitive.

An article in Crossing Cultures, *a publication of the U.S. Department of Health and Human Services, recalled how a major international blunder was successfully avoided when Nancy Reagan revised an earlier decision to bring along her White House china on a state visit to the People's Republic of China in 1984. The Chinese were offended by the implication that China, of all countries, might be deficient in this regard. On the same trip, President Reagan himself fell afoul of the local culture when he offended a shopkeeper by asking him to "keep the change" after paying for a small souvenir, an insult in a country where tips are reserved for lowly servants.*

An expat couple has been invited to an Indian family's home for dinner. They arrive with a bottle of scotch for the host and flowers for his wife. At one point, the wife joins the hostess in the kitchen to ask if there's anything she can do to help. The meal is served in the traditional style, without utensils, and the left-handed expat husband eats with that hand. During the meal the wife, who has chosen mango juice for her beverage, offers a sip to her husband when he asks for a taste.

How has the evening gone? From the Indian point of view, not very well. Some Indians are not allowed alcohol (Muslims and Sikhs, for example); the flowers, on the other hand, would be appreciated in most homes (but not frangipani blossoms, which are only used for funerals). The couple should ask at the door whether it's okay to wear shoes in the house, and even if it is, they should never wear them in the kitchen. But then, guests should always stay in the guest room and not wander around the house. If it's a Brahmin (high-caste) family, the kitchen is sacred and becomes polluted the moment any non-Brahmin enters (and a priest may subsequently have to be called in to perform a purification ceremony). By asking to help (whether she enters the kitchen or not), the spouse may have insulted the family by suggesting they don't have any servants. On the other hand, if there are no servants, it's appropriate to ask. Even the most nontraditional of Indians would be shocked to see someone eating with the left hand, which is used for cleaning oneself after defecating. Finally, drinking from another person's glass or eating from their plate is considered jutho, *unclean, and is never done.*

As in the case of Type I incidents, travel writing is a treasure trove of these kinds of faux pas, and we offer a few examples.

My first shock came when I was requested, politely but firmly, by the guest-master to remove a pair of underpants then flut-

tering happily from the line. This, he pointed out, was a monastery; shirts, socks, handkerchiefs, even vests, might be dried with propriety within its walls. But underpants were a shameful abomination and could on no account be permitted. Meekly, I obeyed; but worse was to come. I woke the following morning at dawn…and made quietly for the wash-house. Its principal furnishing was a huge stone trough; and into this I now clambered, covering myself from head to foot in a deep and luxurious lather. At this point the guest-master appeared. Never have I seen anyone so angry. For the second time in twelve hours I had desecrated his monastery. Having already offended God and the Mother of God with the spectacle of my underpants, I was now compounding the sacrilege by standing stark naked under the very roof of the Grand Lavra. I was the whore of Babylon, I was Sodom and Gomorrah, I was a minion of Satan sent to corrupt the Holy Mountain. I was to put on my scabrous clothes at once and return with all speed to the foul pit whence I had come.

—John Julius Norwich
Mount Athos

I was travelling with a few of the nobles by train. Seeing "Beef" on the menu, I ordered it. The waiter said Beef was Off, so I had something else. Later, back in Dewas, the Maharajah said to me, with great gentleness, "Morgan, I want to speak to you on a very serious subject indeed. When you were travelling with my people you asked to eat something, the name of which I cannot even mention. If the waiter had brought it, they would all have had to leave the table. So they spoke to him behind your back and told him to tell you that it was not there. They did this because they knew you did not intend anything wrong, and because they love you."

—E. M. Forster
The Hill of Devi

A little golden girl of seven [offered me] a coconut. "You shall be blessed," she murmured.... I should have returned her blessing word for word, and after that I should have returned the nut also, for her to take the first sip...; and at last—when I received it back, I should have said "Blessings and Peace" before [drinking]. All I did—woe is me!—was to take it, swig it off, hand it back...empty, with another careless, "Thank you."

"Alas," she said...in a shocked whisper, "...Is that the manners of a young chief of [the white people]?" She told me...the sins I have confessed.... My final discourtesy had been the crudest of all. In handing back the empty nut, I had omitted to belch aloud. "How could I know when you did not belch...that my food was sweet to you? See, this is how you should have done it!" She held the nut towards me...her earnest eyes fixed on mine, and gave vent to a belch so resonant that it seemed to shake her elfin form from stem to stern. "That," she finished, "is our idea of good manners," and wept for the pity of it.

—Arthur Grimble
A Pattern of Islands

A Typical Morning in Cairo

Now let's imagine a typical morning in the life of an expatriate, illustrating the cumulative impact of Type I and Type II incidents on a typical expat. Imagine you're Claire, the female, Cairo-based manager of your company's Middle East region, and your morning goes something like this. You enjoy a quiet breakfast in the sanctity of your home and then begin the drive to work. The streets are thronged with pedestrians, choked with donkey carts, and full of aggressive Egyptian drivers who take regular and prolonged solace in their car horns. You are alternately immobilized by all the confusion and driven to fits of frightening recklessness. You've been told repeatedly that everyone in your position uses a driver, but you're determined to learn how to drive in Cairo; after all, you're going to be living here for three years and you don't want to always be dependent on someone else to get around.

You arrive at the office entrance, where you are smartly saluted by Mustapha, daytime watchman and trusted factotum, who opens your door and then proceeds to "park" your car. Mustapha doesn't really drive so much as he coaxes your car into its narrow parking space at the side of the building. As you walk toward the entrance, you try not to listen for the sound of metal meeting up with stone. Your car has been scraped in this manner twice in the month you've been in Cairo, and Mustapha has denied responsibility both times, blaming the car.

You're served strong Egyptian coffee as soon as you settle at your desk (you've asked twice for a weaker brew) and begin your morning as usual by going over your schedule with your assistant, Yasmina. As this meeting ends, you ask Yasmina if the data you requested yesterday afternoon on El Ghalawi Ltd. has been prepared. She says yes but doesn't offer to bring it. You remind her you're meeting with Khaleed El Ghalawi at 9:30 A.M. and would like to review the information before then. You make a few phone calls, and before you know it, it's 9:30 and Yasmina is announcing Mr. El Ghalawi. When she shows him in, you ask again about the data, but she seems not to hear your question.

Your company is looking for a new shipper to handle its import and export needs, and you are close to reaching an agreement with El Ghalawi Ltd. The discussions and negotiations have gone well up to now, but at the end of your meeting this morning, Khaleed suddenly raises a new issue: he wonders whether you might find it in your heart to create "a small place" on your payroll for two of his cousins. You ask about their background and then explain that you don't have any suitable openings. Khaleed seems embarrassed and immediately drops the matter.

At 10:30 you walk two blocks to keep an appointment at the Ministry of Foreign Trade. You sit down to wait for the man you've come to see, assured by his secretary that he is due any minute, but after forty-five minutes and several more assurances, you decide to leave (and learn later that the man was out of town for the day and, further, knew he was going to be away at the time you originally pressed him for this meeting). On your way back to the office, you stop to buy the *International Herald Tribune,* which the vendor had assured you last night he would have. He doesn't ("God's will," he shrugs). You decide to relax with a coffee in the nearby bakery/cafe. As you try to enjoy a moment of peace and quiet, you're approached and harassed by two insistent male customers, and you decide to retreat to the relative safety of your office. As you leave the cafe, you glance at your watch: 11:45. The whole afternoon awaits you.

Some mornings will be better than others, of course, but most expats get quite an education during the early days of an overseas posting. The problem with cultural incidents is the reactions they provoke in us (Type I) and in the local people (Type II) and, even more importantly, what those reactions *lead to.* Those consequences are the subject of the next chapter, but before we discuss them we need to review our friend's morning and note the emotions it provokes in her and in the people she encounters.

Driving to work in the chaos of rush-hour Cairo, for example, can be frightening and stressful; most people would want to avoid it. But in order to avoid it, you would have to give up your dream of not being dependent on a driver every time you wanted to go somewhere in Egypt. So there's no good choice, and you arrive at the office conflicted and angry at the crazy Egyptians.

Chances are the morning parking ritual with Mustapha will do little to improve your mood. Is it too much to ask that the guy who parks your car should know how to drive? If this happens to be one of the days Mustapha scratches your car and, against all your best instincts, you decide to confront him, his complete denial of any wrongdoing, with the facts (a crumpled fender) staring him in the face, is bound to be deeply frustrating.

The incident with Yasmina is likewise not encouraging. You asked her yesterday to prepare the data on the shipping company, she indicated she would, and she hasn't done it. You ask again, reminding her of the urgency, and you still don't receive it in time. You can't help wondering how you're going to be able to work with her when she doesn't do what she says she will. This is both annoying and worrisome.

The meeting with Khaleed El Ghalawi is also disturbing. You can't bring yourself to hire people you don't need (you'd probably have to hide the fact from headquarters), and you resent what has every appearance of being asked for a bribe. If this is how business is done in this country, you doubt whether you can be effective here.

Then there's the abortive meeting at the Ministry of Foreign Trade and the incident with the newspaper vendor, two more examples of the fact that apparently you can't take people at their word in this country. As someone who has always considered trust fundamental to any successful relationship, you wonder how you're going to manage without it . Finally, there's the harassment at the bakery. It's going to be a long three years if you can't go out by yourself in public.

In a rather short time, our hypothetical expatriate has gone through an impressive inventory of negative emotions: fear, stress, anger, confusion, frustration, annoyance, worry, resentment, doubt, and mistrust. And these incidents, don't forget, are only part of what's happening to our expat every day; she also has to deal with all the problems described in chapter 1. It should be no surprise that as these incidents pile up, triggering reactions like those above, the typical expat begins to develop a negative attitude toward the local people. When that happens, when expats start to turn against the local culture, their chances of succeeding abroad are seriously, perhaps even fatally, undermined.

The Morning Revisited

And that's only *half* the picture. Even as you are reacting left and right to the locals (Type I incidents), they are simultaneously re-acting to you (Type II). While you might be tempted to say that's their problem, it's not that simple. It is their problem in the sense that they're the ones getting annoyed, angry, and frustrated, but it's also your problem if the local people start to turn against you. While they may be the ones feeling offended, you're the one who's going to suffer the consequences. In the end you can't afford to be in Type II incidents any more than you can afford to be in Type I.

If you're wondering just which of the morning's encounters were Type II incidents, take another look at how these events unfolded— this time from the point of view of Mustapha, Yasmina, and the others. Mustapha's not blind; he sees how you cringe every time you turn your car over to him. He dreads these moments even more than you do, though unlike you, he at least tries not to show it. While he does indeed have a driver's license, acquired fifteen years ago after completing a rigorous six-week training and passing his driver's test, as a poor Egyptian and father of six, he can't afford a car and has no friends who can. Thus, he has had almost no opportunity to drive all these years, except for the few agonizing minutes ev-ery morning when he has to park your car. On those two dreadful occasions when he has dented the fender, he expects to be fired. What he doesn't expect is for you to humiliate him in front of the small group that has gathered by asking him if he's responsible. Of course he's responsible; just fire him and get on with it.

Yasmina isn't quite sure what to make of you. She's trying very hard to like you—you're going to be her boss for the next three years, if she can last that long—but things aren't off to a very good start. Late yesterday afternoon, you asked her to pull together some data on a shipping company. She was very polite, but she assumed you weren't serious; surely you know it takes longer than an hour or two to gather that kind of information. She probably should have told you, but she didn't want to be disrespectful and imply that you didn't know what you were talking about. This morning, much to her surprise and embarrassment, you ask her again for the information. She doesn't want to be rude, so she says yes to be polite but clearly signals the data isn't ready by not immediately producing it. If you can't read these signs, what can she do? The last straw is when you ask for the data a third time, embarrassing her in front of Mr. El Ghalawi. Yasmina sits back down at her desk, shaking her head and wondering how you can be so dense.

Mr. Khaleed El Ghalawi is also beginning to wonder about you. Everything seemed fine until this morning when he made the standard request to find a place for a couple of his cousins on your payroll. He's a little surprised, in fact, that he had to bring this matter up; after all, you're the one who's supposed to make the offer, so he doesn't have to look pushy. As a successful businessman, he's obliged to always be looking out for the welfare of the less well-off members of his extended family, and all you have to do is stick these two guys in menial, low-paying jobs where they can't do any harm. He's quite taken aback, incidentally, when you ask about their qualifications; their qualifications are that they're El Ghalawis, and you've just concluded a very favorable business deal with the El Ghalawi family and need to show your gratitude.

On to the Ministry of Trade. What was the man supposed to do, after all, when you insisted on meeting with him on a day he had to be out of town? Did you really expect him to say no? He did say no, of course, when he told you he would have his secretary check his schedule and call you back. When she didn't, that was your answer. When you then called him back, what could he say? He knew you would call the day before to reconfirm, so at least you wouldn't waste your time. When he learned later that you actually came to his office and were surprised and upset that he wasn't there, he just shook his head.

The news vendor doesn't understand you either. You ask him a question about the future, which everybody knows is entirely in God's hands, and then you get upset with *him* when there's no newspaper. As for the men in the bakery/cafe; what are they supposed to think when a woman comes in by herself, makes eye contact, and even smiles? Only one kind of woman ever does that.

Our friend's morning, which she herself knows hasn't gone terribly well, has in fact gone much worse than she realizes. Even as she is beginning to develop negative feelings toward certain local people, they are beginning to develop similar feelings toward her. A process has now been triggered which, if allowed to continue, will greatly complicate and ultimately undermine her overseas experience.

Building a Model of Cross-Cultural Interaction

If we were to build a model of the entire process of crossing cultures, we now have the first two steps.

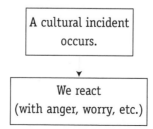

A cultural incident occurs.

We react (with anger, worry, etc.)

The companion model, illustrating the process of cross-cultural interaction from the perspective of the local people (Type II incidents), would be quite similar:

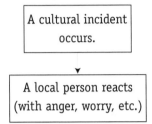

(As we identify additional steps in the process of crossing cultures in later chapters, we will be adding to this model.)

In closing, let's restore a bit of balance to the picture of cross-cultural encounters presented in this chapter. After spending this many pages in the company of people who aren't having much fun together, the reader might have concluded that *all* cross-cultural interactions are doomed to failure, that they inevitably deteriorate into an "incident," whether of Type I or Type II. But this is not the case. While people from different cultures do indeed have different values, beliefs, and behaviors—the ultimate source of all cultural incidents—they will also share various universal values and beliefs, what is commonly called human nature. In other words while people from different cultures are different in *many* respects, they are not different in *all* respects. When they interact, therefore, if their encounter stays within the range of universal behavior (human nature), then no cultural difference will arise and there will be no cultural misunderstanding (though there may still be personal misunderstanding). All intercultural interactions, by their very nature, have the *potential* to turn into cultural incidents, but not all do. If we haven't paid much attention to successful intercultural encounters, it's only because they don't cause problems and don't need fixing. And while they can to some extent mitigate the negative feelings caused by unsuccessful encounters, they cannot prevent them.

The reader should also remember that cultural differences are not the only reason cross-cultural encounters sometimes go wrong. People from different cultures can fail to get along with each other for any number of reasons, of which culture is just one. If you clash with your Egyptian watchman one morning, the reason could be cultural or it could be that one or both of you had a bad night. This is important, for if you attribute every unpleasant encounter you have with a foreigner to a cultural difference, you will not only exaggerate the degree of difference between yours and the local culture, you will also fail to see the real explanation for what went wrong and thus be able to pursue appropriate solutions.

3

The Fallout

The British colony lived what appeared to be a life of blameless monotony rolling about in small cars, drinking at the yacht club, sailing a bit, going to church, and suffering agonies of apprehension at the thought of not being invited to Government House on the Queen's birthday. One saw the murk creeping up over Brixton as one listened to their conversations. Malta and Gibraltar have similar colonies. How often they have been described and how wearisome they are.

—Lawrence Durrell
Bitter Lemons

Intercultural encounters are at the heart of the overseas experience; you can't very well live and work abroad without coming into contact with the local people. When these encounters go wrong, however, and turn into the cultural incidents we have been describing, they become a serious threat to expatriate effectiveness. Unless this threat is met and eliminated, an expat cannot expect to have a successful overseas assignment. In this chapter, we will examine why these cultural incidents are so dangerous, and in chapters 4 and 5 we'll explain how to prevent them.

Turning Against the Local Culture

The most immediate and arguably the greatest danger in cultural incidents is that they cause expats to turn against the local people—and vice versa. As we saw in chapter 2, Type I incidents usually provoke negative reactions in the sojourner (even as Type II incidents provoke similar reactions toward the sojourner from the local people). Expats are put off by the behavior of the locals: it doesn't make any sense; it's counterproductive and inefficient; it's irritating, offensive, and troubling. In a word, it's wrong.

Because of their behaviors, you begin to make negative judgments about the local people: they're lazy and have no ambition; they have no sense of time, don't care about deadlines, and aren't serious about their work; they're dishonest and can't be trusted; they have no work ethic, in fact no ethics of any kind; they just don't understand. If you want something done right, you'd better do it yourself. It's no wonder things don't work in this country.

Once you begin to develop attitudes like these, triggered (don't forget) by cultural incidents, they start to color all your subsequent interactions with the local people. You tend to see only those things which reinforce these attitudes and to overlook behaviors that might give you a more balanced view. You start to expect less and less of the local people and to look for ways to work around them. You begin devising elaborate (often costly) strategems to get things done without involving them, or even deciding not to try certain things because you believe they won't succeed in these circumstances.

Or, alternatively, you may try to get the local people to change some of their ways. While this *can* work, it has to be done with great care and only after you understand why the locals behave the way they do. But most expats who try to "change the way things are done around here" start long before they have even a rudimentary understanding of the culture; they start, in fact, as soon as they begin encountering behaviors they want to change. Any time you try to fix something before you understand how it works, you will only succeed by accident, which is precisely why so many expat schemes for adding value or improving efficiency in overseas operations ultimately fail. When they do fail—largely because of your behavior, by the way, not the locals'—this only confirms the already low opinion you have of the culture.

Once you develop negative attitudes toward the local people, you will naturally want to limit your contact with them. After all, the emotions caused by cultural incidents—anger, fear, worry, frustration, to name just a few—are decidedly unpleasant; if you're like most people, you probably don't enjoy being in these emotional states and instinctively try to avoid them as much as possible. Beyond that, you will likely try to avoid the circumstances that produce these emotions to begin with. This means avoiding or, where that's not possible, minimizing contact with people from the local culture, and for the local people, it means avoiding or minimizing contact with you.

Avoidance seems like it would be a tidy solution to the problem of cultural incidents: if there is no contact, after all, there can be no incident. If there's no incident, there can be no more negativity. The only difficulty, of course, is that even if it were possible to live abroad and not encounter the locals (which it's not), this wouldn't make you very effective. Another difficulty is that avoiding the locals, as we'll see below, does not in fact reduce negativity; in many cases, it actually increases it. In the end, the only real solution to the problem of cultural incidents is to keep them from happening in the first place.

The Foreign Community

Before we look at the dangers of avoidance, we should give it its due. While it may not propel us along the path to cultural effectiveness, it does make sense in certain situations, especially at the beginning of an overseas sojourn. Let's begin by explaining what is meant by avoidance, or, more precisely, what actually happens when expats withdraw from the local people. Quite simply, if you avoid or minimize contact with the locals, it means you either spend your time alone or, more likely, with people from your own country. If the root problem is the "foreignness" of the locals, then surely the antidote is to spend time with people who are not foreign. With people like yourself, after all, there will be no cultural incidents. Effectively, this means spending your time in what is usually referred to as the "expat subculture" (also known variously as the expat community, the foreign community, the foreign colony), a parallel culture, wherein they have achieved the rather dubious distinction of living abroad without ever leaving home. No matter how avoidance begins, this is almost always where it ends.

Perhaps the most famous and most extreme examples of such communities were the British expat compounds in India during the period of the Raj. Rather than live in India, the British colonials chose to bring their world to the subcontinent, constructing uncannily accurate copies of Wiltshire and Devon villages, complete with parade grounds, bandstands (with bands), stone churches, picket fences, gravel walkways, and even golf courses where feasible. There the colonials would cling tenaciously to a lifestyle more passionately British, if the truth be told, than many of them had ever lived back home.

Geoffrey Moorhouse has described the life of expat spouses inside what he calls India Brittanica.

> Discouraged in the first place from making real contact with India and lacking the will to pick up more than a smattering of language adequate for speaking to the servants, the [spouses] became progressively more isolated...[in an] expatriate sub-community of their own. They were renowned

50

for their attempts to reproduce English gardens...in tropical or semi-desert conditions that turned all vegetation either to dust or jungle within a few months.... They waited eagerly for the arrival of catalogues from the big London stores, which reached India towards the end of summer...so that if you moved fast you might expect to order Christmas presents and receive them just in time.

[Their] daily routine went something like this; up at 5 A.M. with horse-riding till 7 A.M.; breakfast on the verandah, followed by a cold bath before dressing to receive visitors at 10 A.M.; anything up to four hours of social chat with the visitors; lunch at 2 P.M. followed by a siesta, which might amount to lying in bed with a book till it was time to ride again and enjoy more social chat or a stroll near the bandstand...after nightfall a supper party, with songs round the pianoforte until bedtime. (1984, 94–95)

Over a hundred years later, official American expats live in a very similar world in the heart of downtown New Delhi. The particulars may be different, but "Americaland," as it's sometimes called, derives from the same set of needs and the same mentality, as we can see in this 1986 *Washington Post* profile of life in the foreign service community there.

Officially referred to as the U.S. Embassy compound, Americaland is nearly self-sufficient, spread over three adjacent complexes and thirty-eight acres. It includes the embassy itself, the ambassador's residence, a school, a four-bed hospital, offices, apartments, a restaurant, a movie theater, a swimming pool, an athletic field, a bowling alley and a barbershop. The commissary sells Kraft mayonnaise, Purina Puppy Chow and Cheerios.

"Every time I leave the compound," says Al Friedbauer, a communications officer...I feel like I'm going into a country I've never been to." (27 November)

For wives the American Women's Association organizes group expeditions into the old city of Delhi to buy jewelry and go sightseeing. "A lot of women don't feel comfortable going out, even shopping, alone," says Diane Hughey, the coordinator of the embassy's Community Liaison Office.

> *Americaland seems to fulfill a certain need. It is a study in how people grapple with culture shock.... Judy Hansen, wife of a World Bank economist, remembers bursting into tears when she couldn't find an open drugstore to buy medicine for strange, itching welts that had appeared on her legs. It was June, 110 degrees. "I came back to the house," she recalls, "and said: I just want to go home. I can't take it anymore."*

52

If you are at all inclined to withdraw from the local culture, as anyone in the throes of country and culture shock surely is, these communities provide the perfect haven. Indeed, even for expats who are not inclined to withdraw, the lure of the expat world is almost irresistible. In their most completely developed form, these communities are the answer to every burned-out, culture-bashing expat's periodic prayer: living abroad without leaving home.

A Safe Harbor

While expat subcultures are a decidedly mixed blessing, at the right moments and in the right dose they serve legitimate, important needs. Every expat, no matter how earnest and sincere about crossing cultures, needs to get away now and then from the craziness of Bangkok or New York. After another day of cultural "experiences"—eight or nine hours of offending and being offended by people, not understanding and not being understood by people, causing scenes, and otherwise making a fool of yourself, and all the while trying very hard to be a sensitive, nonjudgmental, open-minded, and genuinely decent human being—who doesn't need to unwind in a setting where everyone speaks your language, comes from your culture, and thinks you're normal? This isn't avoiding the local culture; it's just resting up from it.

The expat colony can also be a welcome refuge for nonworking spouses who, unlike working expats, have no ready-made structure to slip into overseas or an office full of people waiting to interact with them. They have no structure except what they can cobble together themselves, and no one waiting for them. Moreover, as we noted in chapter 1, spouses typically spend much more time in the local culture than do employees, getting a much bigger dose of country and culture shock. Isolated, lonely, and bored, spouses find an oasis of calm and much-needed companionship and support in the local expat subculture.

There's nothing wrong with wanting to read a newspaper from home, swap stories or compare notes with compatriots, or play a home-country sport that's not played in your overseas post. Expat subcultures can also be a great boon at holiday time, when traditions from home can be celebrated and maintained, and during important rites of passage, when expats feel a special need to connect to their own culture somehow. They also meet a number of important needs of the teenage children of expat families.

If avoidance always leads to spending more time in the expat subculture, that is not altogether a bad thing. At certain times, under certain circumstances, the foreign subculture offers expats a lifeline that keeps them from sinking beneath the weight of all the foreignness around them.

A Mixed Blessing

But there is also a dark side to the typical expat subculture, a side sojourners are well advised to pay attention to. As mentioned above, life in the foreign colony is very tempting, even somewhat restorative, especially during those first few months of country and culture shock. But if the expat is not careful, what starts out innocently enough as an occasional retreat to "the Club" becomes a habitual pattern of behavior that may be impossible to break. You begin to find yourself spending increasingly more time in the company of other expats, no longer out of any particular need but simply out of habit. Where once the expat community was a much-needed safe harbor, it quickly becomes a place to hide out from the local culture. And once underway, the process of withdrawal tends to accelerate, almost as if it were feeding on itself. The more you retreat from the culture and the people, the less you learn about them; the less you know about them, the more uncomfortable you feel among them; the more uncomfortable you feel among them, the more inclined you are to withdraw. Meanwhile, the local culture recedes further and further into the distance, taking with it your chances of becoming an effective expatriate.

"We were in India," an expat recalls in Charles Allen's *Plain Tales from the Raj,*

> we were looked after by Indian servants and we met a great many Indians, and some of us undoubtedly made a very close study of India and Indian customs, but once you stepped inside the home you were back in Cheltenham or Bath. We brought with us in our home lives almost exact replicas of the sort of life that upper middleclass people lived in England at that time.... You went from bungalow to bungalow and you found the same sort of furniture, the same sort of dinner table set, the same kind of conversation. We read the same books, mostly imported by post from England, and I can't really say that we took an awful lot from India. (1984, 82)

Another danger of overdosing on the expat community is the negative, even hostile attitude many members have toward the local culture. There's more than a touch of irony here: people who have the least contact with the locals are often the most critical of them. There's also a certain perverse logic at work. Even as you slip comfortably into the expatriate lifestyle, your conscience is not altogether clear. At some level you realize what's happening, that you have undertaken to trivialize the experience of living abroad and perhaps even to undermine your own professional effectiveness. If you are sincere in your desire to live in and come to know another culture, or even just to succeed in your work, this is probably a realization you'd just as soon avoid.

So you look around for another, more palatable explanation for what has happened, one that fixes the blame elsewhere. And there is one ready to hand: it's not you who has withdrawn from the local culture; it's the local culture that has pushed you away. You really did try, but you just don't approve of so many of the attitudes and behaviors of the local people. For this self-deception to work—and there's a lot riding on it—you have to paint the culture in as bad a light as possible, a task, incidentally, in which you will be enthusiastically joined by numerous other escapees desperately needing to justify their own withdrawal. When it comes to criticizing the local culture, there is great comfort in numbers. This is how avoiding the local people often produces greater, not less, negativity in expats.

The anthropologist Kalvero Oberg, one of the first people to use the expression "culture shock," has described "the hostile and aggressive attitude" toward the locals that many expats develop.

> *This hostility grows out of the genuine difficulty the visitor experiences in the process of adjustment. There is mail trouble, school trouble, language trouble, house trouble, transportation trouble, shopping trouble, and the fact that people in the host country are largely indifferent to all these troubles. You become aggressive, you band together with*

your fellow countrymen and criticize the host country, its ways and its people. This criticism is not an objective appraisal but a derogatory one. You talk as if your experiences are...created by the people of the host country. You take refuge in the colony of your countrymen and its cocktail circuit, which often becomes the fountainhead of emotionally charged...stereotypes. (1981, 22–23)

Criticisms of the host country, "justified" or not, serve no useful purpose. At best they only reassure those who have withdrawn from the culture of the wisdom of their decision, and at their worst they raise doubts in those who are still trying to be open-minded. They are a meal best left untouched.

"My wife got invited one time to a *gringa* [female expats] party," one man remembers of his experience in Mexico.

That was after the day she had met someone in the local Kmart who told her they have a group of twenty-four American women who get together in one another's house once a month to, quote, bitch about these damn Mexicans, unquote.... [But] it was these damn Mexicans who helped us move in, who helped us find our way around town. And now that we were more or less settled, these aristocratic holier-than-thou's show up and decide they want to be our friends. No, thank you. (Osland 1995, 55)

Even those who seek only minimal contact with their compatriots often find themselves pulled into the expat world much more than they intend to be. If it is to survive, the expatriate community has to be worked at; it is something of an illusion, after all, an artificial construct, and illusions, as any actor will tell you, require constant attention. So there are committees and committee meetings, cultural events, amateur theatricals, birdwalks, tennis tournaments, swimming, sculpture, gardening and history classes, barbecues, fund drives, and, of course, charity events. Contact is the lifeblood of these communities, though the quality of the contact is not nearly as important as the frequency. The average expatriate, even if he or she genuinely desires contact with the local people, barely has the time for it. And after a while, the desire gradually dies.

Aldous Huxley wrote of his voyage to Asia in the 1920s.

> *Everyone in the ship menaces us with the prospect of a very good time in India. A good time means going to the races, playing bridge, drinking cocktails, dancing till four in the morning, and talking about nothing. And meanwhile the beautiful, the incredible world [we've come to see] awaits our explorations, and life is short.... Heaven preserve me, in such a world, from having a Good Time! I shall see to it that my time in India is as bad as I can make it.* (1985, 11)

57

In some cases the regulars in the expat community get upset when the "occasionals" try to cut back on or limit their involvement. To "lose" a member to the local culture threatens the solidarity of the community, and an artificial community such as this is nothing without its solidarity. "Some people refused to kowtow to all these social things," one expat observed about his time in Asia, "and refused to belong to the Club.... [But] you were unwise not to become a Club member if you could. If you didn't belong...you were an outcast, a rebel, a rather courageous rebel" (Allen, 117).

Closed Circle

Even for its most enthusiastic adherents, life in the expat community can sometimes be a sterile, unsatisfying proposition. In the end, there is about it the aura of missed opportunities and a failure of will. More often than not what binds its members together is not personal affinity or mutual respect or even common interests but a shared reluctance to delve into the local culture and take what comes. One expat has observed,

> *[Outside] we spent our time watching our step and watch-*
> *ing what we said, and there was a certain relief to go amongst*
> *people of our own race [at the club] and let our hair down.*
> *On almost any evening you would see the club*
> *verandah...occupied by literally hundreds of people in groups*
> *of two, four, and upwards. They would be busily chatting*
> *amongst themselves [and] drinks would be flowing freely....*
> *Within those "basket chair circles" the conversation was said*
> *to be trivial in the extreme. A small community continually*
> *re-meeting could not be very original.* (119, 124)

Members of the expat community don't seek each other out so much as they collide with each other in their common flight from the indigenous culture. The irony is that if they take the time to find out, expatriates often discover they share as many values and interests with the natives they have declined to get to know as with the compatriots with whom they force themselves to fraternize. Peopled with such strange bedfellows, the expatriate community, at its core, is not a true community at all.

"There was my life in the [British] hospital," an expat character writes in Paul Scott's *The Jewel in the Crown*, his masterpiece about the expatriate experience in pre-World War II India,

> *which also included the [all British] club and the boys and*
> *girls and all the good-time stuff that wasn't really good at*
> *all, just the easiest, the least exciting, so long as you ig-*
> *nored the fact that it was only the easiest for the least admi-*
> *rable part of your nature.*
>
> *After a while I began to see that the ease of companion-*
> *ship wasn't really ease at all, because once you had got to*
> *know each other, and had then to admit that none of you*

*really had much in common except what circumstances had
forced on you, the companionship seemed forced itself.* (1979,
385, 404)

Some Caveats

It would be wrong to see the expat subculture as nothing more
than a collection of malcontents trying desperately to rally new-
comers to their dubious cause. While there are indeed malcontents
in most foreign colonies, by and large the expat community is
made up of decent people whose only mistake is not to have tried
a little harder. After all, very few expats deliberately set out to
avoid the local culture and go overseas giddy at the prospect of
meeting scores of their countrymen and spending every weekend
at The Club. Avoidance is, rather, merely an instinctive, self-de-
fensive reaction to unpleasant situations. So if expats do retreat
on occasion into the safety of the foreign community, it's only to
recover from the excesses of country and culture shock. And if
they go back more often and stay longer than they should, this is
rarely because of a conscious, calculated decision to avoid the
local people, but merely the failure to pay enough attention to
how they spend their time. The fact that withdrawing is an uncon-
scious, natural instinct does nothing to mitigate its negative consequences, but it does put expats in a better light. These aren't
bad people; they're good people mixed up in a bad business.

Naturally, the mere existence of the expat community does
not guarantee that all expats will join it, or that all those who do
join it will overindulge, but these are strong possibilities. If you
don't deliberately choose a lifestyle when you live overseas—and
most people aren't in the habit of monitoring their behavior that
closely—human nature is such that you will automatically gravi-
tate toward the familiar, the known, and the comfortable. In the

end, few expats actually choose to live in the expat colony; they simply end up living there because they fail to choose anything else. This is what makes the expat subculture so dangerous—not that expats seek it out, but that it seeks them out.

Many of these same people are the first to admit in retrospect that they missed out on the opportunity of a lifetime. "If I have a regret," one spouse reflected on her experience in New Delhi, "it's that I haven't been able to make [Indian] friends, just to make friends. And that's sad. Because as much as we like India, that would have enhanced our appreciation of it" (*Washington Post* 1986).

The foreign colony lifestyle does not have to be an all-or-nothing proposition: either you stay away from the expat compound and live entirely in the local culture, or you play in tennis tournaments and never speak to the natives. Many expats manage to straddle both worlds quite nicely. This chapter has exaggerated the dangers of withdrawal to bring home the point. In the end, you don't have to choose which world you want to live in; you can live in both. But to do so, you will have to keep your wits about you.

Remember, finally, that not everyone is a born culture-crosser. For any number of reasons, some people who go abroad aren't very good at and may not even be capable of adjusting successfully to a foreign culture, and they do more harm than good if they force themselves to try. Moreover, those who adapt readily enough in one country may not adapt at all in another. For all of these individuals, making a life for themselves in the foreign colony may represent a considerable accomplishment and be the only alternative to going home early. If this describes you, you need not flee the expat subculture or feel somehow obliged to explain your behavior. Even so, try to avoid the trap of criticizing the local people and be alert for opportunities to learn more about their culture.

Adding to the Models

We are now in a position to add a new box to our model of cultural effectiveness begun in chapter 2. With the addition, the process now looks like this:

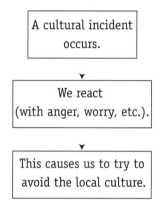

Remember that avoidance, like reaction, is a two-way proposition, that the entire dynamic described in this chapter is also happening in the other direction. Even as you are reacting to and trying to avoid the local people, the locals are likewise reacting to your behavior and trying to minimize contact with you. And just as you swap stories about the annoying locals, locals complain about the annoying foreigners. Thus the chasm between you and the local culture widens from both sides. We need to add the avoidance component to our companion model of crossing cultures (illustrating the process from the local perspective), which now looks like this:

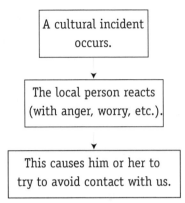

A cultural incident occurs.

The local person reacts (with anger, worry, etc.).

This causes him or her to try to avoid contact with us.

The frequency of expat-to-local contact is much greater than local-to-expat contact, of course, meaning the chasm widens faster from the expat side. An individual expat is surrounded by the local culture and has numerous encounters with the local people every day. The typical local person, on the other hand, probably only interacts with a handful of expats on a regular basis, and most locals interact with expats only occasionally. Expats, then, are likely to experience considerably more cultural incidents during any given period than are the locals and to feel, therefore, a greater urgency to escape. In the end, from whichever direction and in whatever ways the divide widens, it's not a positive development.

Note also that your withdrawal from the local culture does not go unremarked. Observant locals can't help but notice if you seem to keep your distance and socialize largely with other expats. They note—and before long they begin to accommodate—your preferences. For this reason, even as you withdraw from the locals, the locals become less inclined to seek you out. "It would be better if they went to church," an Eskimo says of the development workers who live with the natives in Canada's far north,

> even if they could not understand. It would show that they
> had some interest in what is happening in the settlement.

Perhaps some problems would not arise if the Whites both-
ered to go to church with the Eskimos; maybe they would
understand things better. It would make the people think
that the Whites belong to the settlement. (Brody 1975, 170)

This, then, is where the overseas experience of many expats stalls, trapped in a kind of perpetual tension between the clear and obvious need to interact with locals and a strong desire not to because of the unpleasantness of those very interactions. If you aspire to be truly effective in your overseas assignments, you must break through this impasse and get beyond the temptation to withdraw from the local culture.

4

The Problem Explained

The first thing an Englishman does on going abroad is to find fault with what is French, because it is not English.
—William Hazlitt
Notes of a Journey Through France and Italy

In chapter 3 we saw that it is possible to avoid cultural incidents, alas, at the cost of being less effective in an overseas assignment. Avoidance is thus not a true solution to the problem of such encounters. In the final analysis, the only true solution to these incidents is to keep them from happening in the first place, and in this chapter we will take the first and most important step in that process: we will look at what *causes* cultural incidents.

Let's return to one of the Type I incidents from chapter 2, the vignette of the American posted in Argentina:

You're an American expatriate working in Buenos Aires. You have a 10:00 A.M. appointment with the Argentinian manager of a local public relations firm, and it's now 10:30. The receptionist tells you the person you've come to see is meeting with someone else. You wait another half an hour, during which time another person (who has the next appoint-

ment?) arrives. At 11:00 the manager emerges from his of-
fice to greet you. To your amazement, he neither acknowl-
edges nor apologizes for making you wait an hour. You find
this behavior extremely rude and are furious with him.

Why is the American put off by the Argentinian's behavior? The
short answer is because it's not "normal," not what people are
supposed to do in such situations, and when people don't do what
they're supposed to, other people get upset. But why is the Argentinian supposed to apologize for making the American wait? Because that's what an American would do in this situation. In other
words, the American is angry because he expects the Argentinian
to behave the way Americans do.

66

The Ethnocentric Impulse

It is precisely this belief, *that other people are like us*, that is the
source of most cross-cultural incidents. If we truly believe other
people are like us, then it's only natural to expect them to behave
the way we do (the origin of Type I incidents) and to assume that
we behave the way they do (the origin of Type II incidents). Look
again at all the incidents in chapter 2. You will see that in every
case the problem is the same: the person from Culture A was expecting the person from Culture B to behave like people from Culture A. When that person did not, when the person in fact be-
haved like people from Culture B, there was trouble.

But why should this be? Why would we expect other people to
behave like us? The answer, quite simply, is because they always
have. That is, most of us grow up in circumstances where we are
surrounded by people from our own culture, and while we might
have occasional contact with someone from a different culture,
most of our interactions are with people like ourselves. And the
reason these people are like us, of course, is that from birth we

have been carefully and deliberately raised to be *like them*.

This is the phenomenon known as cultural conditioning wherein members of a particular group teach the next generation how to behave and how to function effectively and thereby survive in that group or culture. The adults (parents, teachers, and others) teach the code of conduct of that particular society, which stipulates what people should and should not do across the entire spectrum of interpersonal interactions. Children are rewarded when they do the right thing and punished when they do not, and what makes those things right or wrong are the values and beliefs of that particular culture.

Another word for the right and wrong behaviors we learn through our cultural conditioning is *norms,* from which we derive our word *normal*. The essential fact to grasp about norms is that they not only make it easier to interact with other people—they make it possible. If there were no norms, if we could not rely on people to always behave in certain ways in certain situations, human interaction would be hopelessly unpredictable and chaotic. If we could not be sure, for example, that drivers would stay on their side of the road, always stop when required, and turn left only from the left-hand lane, we would surely hesitate to drive. "Staying comfortable," Edward Hall has written, "is largely a matter of culture. Informal or core culture is the foundation on which interpersonal relations rest. All of the little things that people take for granted...depend on sharing informal patterns" (1984, 195).

In the end, we do not merely *expect* other people to be like us; thanks to our cultural conditioning, we *depend* on it. Thus it is that the same conditioning which can make it so difficult for us to function overseas is what makes it possible for us to function at home. Is it any wonder we cling to it?

Because of our cultural conditioning, we not only think our actions are normal, the way everyone behaves; we also think what we do is right, the way everyone *should* behave. We therefore regard any behavior that is different from ours as wrong. Naturally, this puts cultural incidents into a whole new light. When the locals do something that causes an incident, they're not simply behaving in a way we're not expecting; they're behaving in a way we don't approve of. Thus do values enter the cross-cultural dynamic and considerably raise the ante in cultural incidents. It's no secret that where values are concerned, people have very strong views, and when very strong views are in play, emotions run rampant—all the more reason, then, to get to the bottom of cultural incidents and learn how to prevent them.

Up to the moment you go abroad or otherwise have a significant encounter with people from another culture, you have no reason or basis for believing that other people, *including foreigners,* might not behave like you—for believing that some of the norms you've picked up over the years might be peculiar to your particular group or society. You have no idea, in short, that what is normal to you is not also universal, that much of what you think of as human nature is only cultural.

But what happens when you encounter someone from a different culture, someone raised with different conditioning and a different set of norms? How do you expect that person to behave? By now, the answer should be obvious: if you have not been raised in that culture or have had only limited contact with that culture, then you would expect that person to behave in the only way you've ever known other people to behave: like you. That may be very ethnocentric of you, but ethnocentrism is a fundamental fact of the human condition. Hickson and Pugh have written,

> [W]e are all subject in our thinking, at least to some degree, to "ethnocentrism." [This] is the implicit assumption, often unawares, that our culture is the best, that our way of doing things is normal, the right way.... We all overestimate

the importance of our country and our culture in the scheme of things. When we see something different in another culture, we are liable to view it as abnormal and inferior....

The development of this belief in our own culture is an important part of our ability to function effectively in it. But it is a feature of human nature which does lead to problems when we come to operate in other cultures. (1995, 253–54)

Logic versus Instinct

But there's something wrong here, isn't there? Surely in the age of globalization and cross-cultural training we all know better, that the world is home to a great variety of people and cultures, many of them nothing at all like us. Indeed, isn't one of the reasons we want to go abroad in the first place to encounter and learn about another culture? How is it possible to be steeped in the notion of cultural differences and at the same time assume everyone else is just like us?

In fact, we *do* know better than to expect foreigners to behave like us. But that knowledge doesn't make any difference. What we know to be true (or right or best) is not always what drives our actions. What the conscious intellect tells us—in this case, that foreigners are surely *not* like us—is no match for what a lifetime of cultural conditioning has taught us. For the notion of cultural differences to take deep and lasting root in our psyche, it must be constantly reinforced over a sustained period until it is internalized. Until that time, it's entirely possible—indeed, it's inevitable—that we can cheerfully subscribe to the view that foreigners are different and still be stunned the first time we see a Hindu drink cow urine.

To put all this another way, what we have actually experienced, what we know to be real, will always have more truth for us, more claim on our emotions, than what we've only read or heard about. Moreover, what we've experienced repeatedly will always seem truer than what we've experienced only once or twice. "Of the fact that it takes all sorts to make a world I have been aware ever since I could read," Aldous Huxley has written,

> But proverbs are always platitudes until you have experienced the truth of them. The newly arrested thief knows that honesty is the best policy with an intensity of conviction that the rest of us can never experience. And to realize that it takes all sorts to make a world one must have seen a certain number of the sorts with one's own eyes.
>
> There is all the difference in the world between believing academically, with the intellect, and believing personally, intimately, with the whole living self. (1985, 207)

So perhaps it isn't logical to assume other people are like us, but we're not operating here at the level of logic. We're operating, rather, at the level of instinct, and logic never wins in a fair fight with instinct. "Truth is not that which can be demonstrated by the aid of logic," Antoine de Saint Exupery has observed. "Let logic wangle its own explanation of life" (1967, 187).

We shouldn't be too hard on expats, then. The fact that they expect the locals to behave like them is not something expats dream up just in time to go overseas. Nor is it something they decide to do or are even consciously aware of doing. It's merely something they've done all their lives—in order to survive. It just happens to be something that doesn't serve them very well overseas.

Imagining the Other

The capacity of the average person to fully conceive of the "other" has always been greatly exaggerated. It is interesting in this context, and also quite instructive, to reflect on so-called science fiction, on the people who are in the business of creating Not Us. Even these people, whose job it is to imagine the "other," aren't very successful. Who doesn't know the famous bar scene in the film *Star Wars,* where Luke Skywalker, Obiwan Kenobe, and Chewbacca visit a local watering hole in search of an experienced pilot. The place is teeming with a wondrous variety of extraterrestrial bad guys. But when you think about it, they're not really *that* extraterrestrial. Oh, they may have a second head, some additional arms, and more eyes than you or I, but that's just it: they have *more* of these attributes (or sometimes fewer) but they don't have *different* attributes, something *instead* of heads, arms and eyes. They're just variations on a theme—humans—but not a new piece of music. Nor have the film-makers come up with anything new, anything nonhuman, for these guys to do. They're just doing what guys like them everywhere do, apparently even in other galaxies: knocking back a few at the local neighborhood hangout. Not even George Lucas and Steven Spielberg can conceive of nonhuman behavior; there are no models. Most of us even conceive of animals in human terms, explaining their behavior exclusively in reference to our own.

71

The science fiction writer Ursula Le Guin makes just this point in her classic novel *The Left Hand of Darkness.* One of her human characters observes about an alien,

> *When you meet a Gethenian, you cannot and must not do what a [human] naturally does, which is to cast him in the role of Man or Woman, while adopting towards him a corresponding role dependent on your expectations of the patterned or possible interaction between persons of the same or opposite sex. Our entire pattern of socio-sexual interaction is nonexistent here. They cannot play the game. They do not see one another as men or women. This* is almost impossible for our imagination to accept. *What is the first question we ask about a newborn baby?* (emphasis author's) (1977, 94)

The old proverb notwithstanding, we cannot put ourselves in someone else's shoes. Or, more accurately, we can, but it's still our own feet that we feel.

A New Step

We're now ready to add an important new step at the beginning of our model of cross-cultural interaction, the behavior that sets this whole process in motion.

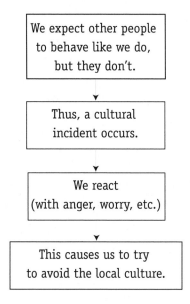

As noted earlier, the conviction that everyone is the same is the cause of both Type I and Type II incidents. It creates Type I incidents because it means we are bound to get upset when the local people don't behave like we do. And it creates Type II incidents because it means the locals are bound to get upset when we don't behave like they do. The only difference between the two types is in who is doing the expecting and who is getting upset. So we can also add a very similar new box to our companion model of the process of crossing cultures.

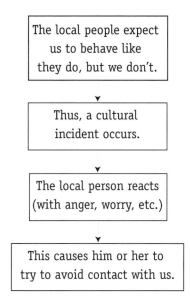

Strictly speaking, the local people are ultimately responsible for Type II incidents; the true cause of these incidents, after all, is the locals' belief that we will behave like they do. But our own ethnocentrism does contribute *indirectly* to Type II incidents, in the sense that if we believe everyone else is like us, then we must believe, as a natural corollary, that we are like everyone else. And if *we* don't find anything odd in our own behavior, then why would the locals? You don't think this all out, of course, but it does naturally follow from the basic ethnocentric premise. As we shall see in the next chapter, if you can break the grip of ethnocentrism, you can solve the riddle of both Type I and Type II incidents.

5

The Problem Solved

The born traveller—the man who is without prejudices, who sets out wanting to learn rather than to criticize, who is stimulated by oddity, who recognizes that every man is his brother, however strange and ludicrous he may be in dress and appearance—has always been comparatively rare.
> —Hugh and Pauline Massingham
> *The Englishman Abroad*

Now that we've identified the cause of cultural incidents—the assumption that other people are like us—it should be clear, at least in a general way, how to prevent them: we have to stop making this erroneous assumption. How to do that is the subject of this chapter.

As we begin, we need to look a bit closer at the idea that our assumption of cultural sameness is what causes cultural incidents. If this is true, then ultimately it is not the behavior of the local people that causes cultural incidents but our own. The problem is not what the local people do, but the fact that *we are expecting them* to do something else. In other words, our expectation, not their behavior, is the real sticking point.

This is in fact very good news for the culture crosser. If the reverse were true, if the cause of cultural incidents was the behavior of the local people, then the solution would be for them to somehow change their behavior. And that's not going to happen. But if the problem is actually our own behavior, then there's hope, for while we can't very well expect the local people to change their behavior to conform to our expectations, we may be able to change our expectations to conform to their behavior.

The Starting Point

In general, then, the way to prevent cultural incidents is to stop assuming that other people are like us. If we didn't expect the local people to behave like we do, we would no longer be critical when they didn't. If we were no longer put off by their behavior, there would be no more cultural incidents (of Type I, anyway), and if there were no more incidents, it would not be so difficult to be culturally effective.

To stop expecting other people to behave like we do is actually a two-step process: first we have to realize that we have this expectation, and second we have to start expecting the local people to simply be themselves.

The first step, realizing we expect others to be like us, is in many ways the most difficult, for it requires that we somehow become aware of behavior that is completely subconscious. Indeed, this particular expectation, as we saw in the previous chapter, is in fact a deep-seated survival instinct, and instincts (as we saw in that same chapter) are notoriously difficult to get hold of.

It so happens, however, that we have readily to hand a foolproof mechanism for raising this particular instinct to the level of conscious awareness: it is none other than that frustration, surprise, or anger that arises in us at the time a cultural incident occurs. These emotions are triggered precisely at the moment the locals fail to do what we expect; thus, if we could somehow train ourselves to become aware of these emotions, then we would by that very act be catching ourselves in the process of expecting the locals to behave like we do. When that happens, when you see yourself making this assumption—in complete defiance of all logic and in complete thrall to your cultural conditioning—it is deeply sobering. If you then combine awareness of this counterproductive behavior with an appreciation of its damaging consequences and with the further realization that *you* are responsible for this whole process—if you connect all these dots, you won't think much of the resulting picture. Thus put off by your own behavior, you're ready to do something about it.

The key to this whole dynamic, as noted earlier, is to somehow become aware of your emotional reactions to cultural incidents. But awareness of emotional states actually runs counter to most people's experience; they are, rather, in the habit of *having* emotions, of experiencing their feelings, not taking note of them. You are used to being subject *to* your emotions, but not to subjecting those emotions to conscious observation. So awareness is a practice that will have to be consciously enforced against opposing tendencies.

The best way to become aware of your reactions to cultural incidents is to schedule a time during or at the end of every day when you deliberately try to recall moments when you were upset or agitated by something a local person did. As you reconstruct these incidents, you will see yourself, if only after the fact, in the act of expecting other people to behave like you do. Over time and with repeated practice, you should eventually reach the point of simultaneous awareness, when you will be able to observe your emotional reactions to cultural incidents as they occur. You should definitely keep this goal in mind and strive for it. But whether you become aware of your emotions at the time of such incidents or in retrospect, the effect is the same: the realization that it is ultimately *your own behavior* that makes you culturally ineffective. When you begin to see that your cross-cultural wounds are largely self-inflicted, you will then be motivated to take the final step to cultural effectiveness: to start expecting the local people to be themselves.

Filling the Information Gap

Awareness, then, brings us to the brink of solving the problem of cultural incidents. All you need now is some information about the local culture. You can't very well expect to recognize when the locals are behaving like locals if you have no knowledge of how the locals typically behave. You can learn about the local culture in three ways: through observing the locals in action, through asking them about specific behaviors, and through reading about or taking classes in the local culture.

Observing—Not as Easy as it Might Seem

Naturally, if you're able to observe how the local people behave in any given situation, you will then know what to expect from them in similar situations in the future. While this sounds simple enough, this kind of observation is neither as easy nor as straightforward as it may seem. This is because it's not possible to react to and closely observe a situation at the same time; in fact, the former effectively precludes the latter. It's well known, for example, that people rarely remember what happens during moments of great emotional intensity, when they're in danger, let's say, or in a rage. People don't think in such circumstances (much less observe); they simply act out of sheer instinct. When they are asked later what they did, there are periods about which they can recall nothing.

So it will be with you in the midst of many cultural incidents. While your emotional reactions won't normally be as intense as those mentioned above, the basic principle still applies: agitated, angry, frustrated by the unexpected and "abnormal" behavior of a local person, you are not able to see very much of what happens after the triggering behavior has occurred. Prevented in this manner from being able to observe, you not likely to take from such incidents cultural information about what to expect next time.

If we look again at the example of the American expat in Buenos Aires from the last chapter, we can figure out what this man might have been able to see if he had not been so busy getting upset. If he had seen some of these things, they would have given him important clues about Argentinian behavior, not enough to crack the code of the culture, perhaps, but enough to get him thinking differently.

> *You're an American expatriate working in Buenos Aires. You have a 10:00 A.M. appointment with the Argentinian manager of a local public relations firm, and it's now 10:30. The receptionist tells you the person you've come to see is meeting with someone else. You wait another half an hour, during which time another person (who has the next appointment?) arrives. At 11:00 the manager emerges from his office to greet you. To your amazement, he neither acknowledges nor apologizes for making you wait an hour. You find this behavior extremely rude and are furious with him.*

To begin with, the American might have noticed that the receptionist did not seem at all concerned when her boss did not emerge from his office on time to greet his guest. He might have noticed that she was not looking at her watch and, furthermore, that she did not take the initiative to apologize for her boss or otherwise reassure the American that it would not be much longer. If there was something wrong here, something the American should have been reacting to, surely the receptionist would have been agitated as well. Moreover, when the person with the next appointment arrived, the appointment after the American's, the American might also have noticed that this person did not seem concerned that the schedule was apparently backed up, that the receptionist again offered no explanation or apology, and that the new arrival wasn't glancing at her watch or otherwise acting inconvenienced. Finally, the American might have noticed that when the Argentinian did eventually emerge from his office, he offered no apology or explanation to either of the two people waiting for him.

As noted above, the American misses many of these things because he is in fact too upset to see them. If observation is to work for the American, he has to first stop reacting emotionally to cultural incidents and learn to observe his reactions to them as those reactions arise. He can then cut those emotions off and, in the calm that follows, truly observe what's happening around him. He will still miss some things, incidentally (see below for details), but he will at least be on his way toward more objective observation. "To have your eyes widened and your organ of belief stretched," Philip Glazebrook has written,

> whilst remaining discreetly submissive, seems to me a faculty the tourist ought to cultivate.... When you have submitted to looking about you discreetly and to observing with as little prejudice as possible, then you are in a proper state of mind to walk about and learn from what you see. (1984, 181–82)

Some Problems with Seeing

Observation across cultures is notoriously difficult for another reason: there's a great deal you will be unable to see, whether or not you're in the proper state to observe. The trouble is that you will not be able to see anything that does not constitute *meaningful behavior* in your own culture. You must remember in this context that it is not the eyes that see but the mind. The eyes merely convey images to the mind, which then interprets and confers meaning on those images it recognizes, things it has "seen" before, and confers no meaning on—and therefore does not see—anything it does not recognize. In some cultures, for example, pulling on the earlobe is a gesture that warns other people that the person speaking cannot be trusted. If you come from such a culture, this action constitutes meaningful behavior, and you would be capable of seeing it. But if you do not come from a culture where pulling on an earlobe has meaning, then the gesture doesn't constitute behavior and you wouldn't be able to see it and, hence, learn from it. Would you understand, watching a Hindu friend arrange his bedroll, that he was trying to position himself so as not to be pointing his feet at anyone's head (instead of trying to get near the window or away from the door)? "He knew nothing yet well enough to see it," C. S. Lewis writes of one of his characters in *Out of the Silent Planet*; "[Y]ou cannot see things until you know roughly what they are" (1965, 41–42). Edmund Taylor observes,

> *It is one of my regrets that I have not yet learned to see an Indian village or a bazaar; my eyes aren't trained, and I couldn't describe one to save my life. I love them and am endlessly fascinated; but all I can make out is a wild surrealist confusion of men and animals and many kinds of inanimate objects, arranged in completely implausible patterns.* (1964, 67)

How much of the following would you see at a tea shop along the trail in the Himalayas if you didn't already know what was happening? Would you notice that your porter, from a low caste, doesn't actually enter under the roof of the shop but sits just outside (because low caste people aren't allowed inside the building)? Would you notice that the lady handing out the tea lets you take your cup from her hand but sets the porter's on the ground in front of him (lest her hands touch those of a low caste person)? Would you notice that she cleans your cup herself but pours water into his, lets him rinse it out once and set it on the ground, then pours more water in and rinses it out a second time herself? Would you notice, handing your porter a box of matches, that he doesn't take them from you but cups his hands to receive them? Most of these actions would have no meaning for you and would thus be imperceptible. "It is a repeated finding," Edward Stewart notes, "that perceptual responses are influenced by the individual's expectations. To an extent not usually recognized, perception resides in the perceiver, not in the external world" (1972, 15).

Another limitation of cross-cultural observation is that you will often misinterpret what you see. There are many behaviors that mean something both in your own and in the local culture, but not the same thing. Because these behaviors mean something in your culture, you will be able to see them when they are exhibited by someone in the local culture, but you will most likely assign them an incorrect meaning. In India, for example, shaking one's head from side to side, which means no in many Western cultures, means yes. In the South Pacific, belching after a meal (rude in the West) is how people express appreciation of the food. In the Middle East, men who are good friends (and nothing more) walk hand in hand in the street. Clearly, what you "learn" from this kind of observation has limited value and can be quite misleading.

As a means of learning about another culture, of gathering the information that will form the basis of accurate expectations about the local people, observation clearly has its limitations. By itself then, observation is not an entirely reliable source of cultural knowledge, but if it is used critically and in conjunction with the other two sources mentioned earlier in this chapter, talking to the locals and studying about the culture, it is a perfectly respectable technique for learning.

Two Other Methods for Gathering Information

Talking to the local people would seem to be the surest way to learn about their culture; when you want to know something, go to the experts. And this is by and large the case, especially if what you seek is the kind of information we've been talking about here, the specifics of *what* the local people will do in various situations. But if you want to know more, and especially if you want to know *why* they act the way they do (we'll see in a moment why this is important), then the local people can only get you so far. While they generally know what they would do in most common situations, the local people are often among the last to know why they behave that way. After all, the people from a culture are the least likely to have ever observed or thought about their actions. They've had very little occasion to, for one thing, and no ready vantage point for another. Only if they have lived outside their culture would they have had the opportunity of actually seeing it (as every expat can attest).

The third way to learn about the local culture is to study it, through reading or perhaps through a class or intercultural training program. In these contexts you will learn not only how the locals behave in various situations—and be able to adjust your expectations accordingly—but also why they do these things, the basic values, beliefs, and assumptions that lie behind people's behavior and ultimately explain it.

These, then, are the three common ways to learn about the local culture: observation, conversation, and study. And you need to remember that it is learning about the local culture that makes possible the final step in the process of becoming culturally effective: expecting the local people to behave like themselves. In practice you will typically combine all three methods to educate your-self about the locals, using information from one source to verify or complement information you have learned from another. It is wise, in fact, to check all cultural information in this manner and not accept any one source as being definitive. Whether it's your own observation, the views of a local person, or information from a book or workshop, keep in mind that all sources are to some degree subjective.

Completing the Model

We are ready now to complete the model of intercultural interaction we have been building over the last four chapters. Assuming you plan to follow the advice in this chapter, we can now remove the step of cultural avoidance and adjust the graphic accordingly. The process of becoming culturally effective, from beginning to end, now looks something like the model on page 85.

Models like this make a tidy, irresistible package, but they are necessarily simplistic. These *are* the steps a person goes through in becoming culturally effective, but the actual experience is some-what messier. While the general trend is certainly in the direction indicated, the process proceeds in fits and starts. It's not likely, for example, that one day you will be expecting your Italian accountant to behave like you, and the next day, because you read something somewhere, you'll be expecting him to behave like an Italian.

The actual process whereby an expat replaces incorrect, eth-nocentric expectations with culturally appropriate ones is slow and gradual. What usually happens is that as you learn various bits about Italian culture, you gradually begin to have accurate expectations in some situations (those you are in the most often), but you will continue to have the wrong expectations in other situations. Moreover, if for some reason you are not in a certain situation for an extended period, you may forget what you learned

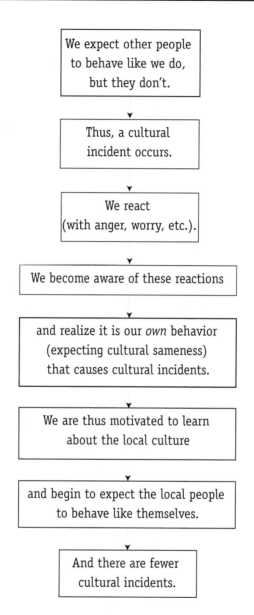

We expect other people
to behave like we do,
but they don't.

Thus, a cultural
incident occurs.

We react
(with anger, worry, etc.).

We become aware of these reactions

and realize it is our *own* behavior
(expecting cultural sameness)
that causes cultural incidents.

We are thus motivated to learn
about the local culture

and begin to expect the local people
to behave like themselves.

And there are fewer
cultural incidents.

and revert to ethnocentric expectations the next time you are in a similar situation. Generally speaking, you will become more effective at those cultural interactions in which you are involved repeatedly and still be reacting to situations with which you are unfamiliar.

But you are now firmly on the path to cultural effectiveness. As your knowledge increases, you will experience fewer incidents. The fewer the incidents, the less inclined you will be to avoid the local people. The more you interact with the local people, the more your knowledge will increase.

Preventing Type II Incidents

Learning about the local culture is also the solution to Type II incidents (wherein it is your behavior that upsets the locals). As you learn how the local people behave in various situations, you are perforce learning how they expect other people (including you) to behave in those situations. If you know what's expected of you and if you are willing and able to behave accordingly, then you will no longer commit Type II incidents.

As seen and experienced from the local point of view, the model of cross-cultural interaction would now be greatly modified and look something like this:

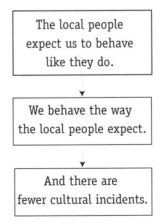

Many expats try to keep from committing Type II errors by reading books on local manners and customs, studying what's usually referred to as the do's and don'ts of the local culture (and much cross-cultural training also includes such lists). This information can indeed save you from embarrassing moments and more serious faux pas, but it should not be the only arrow in your quiver. Lists of do's and don'ts can't cover all contingencies, of course, and tend to greatly oversimplify cross-cultural effectiveness. And this simplicity is, of course, what makes lists so appealing. By all means consult such books, and then go on to other sources to deepen your understanding of underlying cultural values and beliefs.

"It is appropriate," Edward Stewart and Milton Bennett have written in the second edition of *American Cultural Patterns: A Cross-Cultural Perspective*,

> *to consider the possibility of providing Americans going abroad, or foreigners in the United States, with a list of dos and don'ts. Why not tell Americans never to point their feet at a person in Thailand, not to pat a child on the head in Laos, always to use polite and flowery expressions in Saudi Arabia, and not to expect punctuality in Guatemala? In short it should be possible to draw up a list of behaviors ranging from those that are desirable to those that are taboo. This approach is misleading for two major reasons.*
>
> *The evaluation of behavior as desirable or taboo pursues the elusive goal of objectivity. Behavior is concrete but ambiguous: the same action may have different meanings in different situations, so it is necessary to identify the context of behavior and the contingencies of action before sojourners can be armed with prescriptions for specific acts. Fulfillment of this strategy is impossible since the enumeration of possible events is [unlimited]. (1991, 15)*

You may think the local people will tell you when you have made a faux pas and imagine that this is how you will avoid committing Type II incidents. But this isn't likely. For one thing, locals will assume you understand their culture (the ethnocentric impulse) and that you are knowingly behaving badly. Even if they think

87

you don't understand their culture, they're not likely to embarrass you by pointing out that people in their country never do what you've just done (anymore than you would embarrass an expat in your own country in this manner). It may not seem fair, but the onus of learning how to behave in the local culture falls squarely on the guest, not on the host.

Complications

The solution to dealing with cultural incidents described in these pages works in the vast majority of cases, but it does not work in all. Expecting the locals to behave the way they do does take the sting out of most cross-cultural encounters, but there are instances when knowing what the locals are going to do is not enough to prevent you from reacting. In some cases, in other words, the problem with a cultural incident is that it's unacceptable. In these latter cases, knowing the behavior is coming does very little to prevent an emotional reaction.

The behavior of people in other cultures tends to fall into three broad categories. There are many things the locals do that you admire and may even adopt for yourself, none of which, needless to say, provoke a cultural incident. There are many other local behaviors that are not what you would do in that situation but that you can nevertheless learn to live with. These are the behaviors that often lead to cultural incidents and that respond best to the technique outlined in these pages. A key characteristic of these behaviors is that by and large they do not have an ethical or moral dimension at odds with your own; that is, the shock these behaviors produce, the reason they cause an emotional reaction, is because they are abnormal, not because they are immoral. While it may be annoying for an Argentinian businessman not to apologize for keeping an American businessman waiting, it's certainly not unethical or immoral. And the same goes for Germans who keep their doors closed, for Indian software programmers who say they've understood your instructions when they have not, or for your French friend who neglects to introduce you to one of her friends on the street. (See the list of Type I incidents in chapter 2 for other examples.)

The third category of local behavior can be much more troubling. These are behaviors that violate (or at least seem to violate) values so fundamental to your identity and sense of self-esteem that you must reject them. Whether expected or not, these behaviors always create a cultural incident, and usually a serious one. These behaviors will upset you from the day you arrive in the host country to the day you leave, no matter how much you learn about the culture in the meantime. You may get used to them and learn to expect them but you will never fail to react to them, albeit less over time, and you will never approve of them. (Be aware, by the way, that certain of your own behaviors no doubt fall into this same category as far as the locals are concerned.)

Behavior in this third category can be further subdivided into two types, and it is important not to confuse them. One type is incidents that appear to violate your sense of right and wrong but that upon further analysis do not, and the other type is incidents that genuinely violate your moral principles. The latter deserve their status as intractable cultural incidents, but the former stand wrongly accused. Let's take the example of the Indian programmers from chapter 2:

> *You're a European software engineer managing a team of Indian programmers in charge of developing and testing an important new application. You have an imminent deadline and have just explained to your team how to fix a new bug that has been detected. When you ask the team if they have understood your explanation, they say yes and return to their cubicles. The next day, when you check on them, they*

have made no progress whatsoever, and it turns out they did not understand your explanation. You've lost twenty-four hours you can't afford to lose and are not happy.

At first glance it appears the Indian programmers have lied to you; they said they understood your explanation when they did not. If this happens to be behavior you find unacceptable, then you won't be able to solve this incident simply by learning to expect Indians to deceive you in the future. But if you take the time or otherwise have the opportunity to learn more about this particular behavior, you may find that it's not really lying in the Indians' context, and therefore not offensive after all. The first thing you might learn is that yes can mean something very different to Indians than it does to you, that it is not necessarily an affirmation or indication of agreement but merely a polite, ritualistic response to most questions. You might learn further that in Indian culture to say you have not understood an explanation reflects badly on the person doing the explaining (that would be you) and causes him or her to lose face, especially if that person is an authority figure. Finally, you may find (as is the case with many Indians) that subordinates are often very nervous about taking too much of a manager's time and will not want to ask for clarification if they haven't understood something. Bosses are supposed to know this, of course, and are expected to follow up any explanations by coming by the workstation a short time later to see if people are performing as instructed. If they are not, the boss should offer another explanation. But it's not up to subordinates to ask.

If your inquiries yield this kind of cultural information, you will probably be inclined to revise your conclusion that the Indians were lying to you and be able to accept this behavior the next time around. In this particular case, then, behavior that appeared to offend your sense of right and wrong turned out, after you had acquired more cultural knowledge, not to be that offensive after all, turned out, in other words, not to be a true cultural incident.

Unacceptable Behaviors

But cultural knowledge will not always be able to "explain away" the behavior of the local people and thereby neutralize cultural incidents. There will be some cases where even when you know why the local people are behaving the way they are—when you can see, for example, that while their behavior is offensive or shocking to you, it would not be so to them—even in such cases you may still be upset and offended by their actions. These cases will not respond to any amount of cultural explanation and will always create a Type I cultural incident.

Let's take the example of our English friend in the bakery in Cairo. The reader may remember that the hapless Claire retreated to the peace and quite of a Cairo bakery to lick her wounds after a busy morning of cultural incidents, only to become victim to one more incident when two male customers began to harass her. There is, of course, an explanation for this, as Fatima Mernissi observes in the following passage from *Beyond the Veil*:

> *Moslem sexuality is a territorial one, a sexuality whose regulatory mechanisms consist primarily of a strict allocation of space to each sex and an elaborate ritual for resolving the contradictions arising from the inevitable interferences between spaces. Apart from the ritualized trespasses of women into public spaces which are, by definition, male spaces, there are no accepted patterns for interactions between unrelated men and women....*
>
> *Women using public spaces, trespassing on the male universe, are restricted to a few occasions and bound by specific rituals such as the wearing of the veil.... The veil means that the woman is present in the men's world, but invisible; she has no right to be in the street.*

> Women in male spaces are considered provocative and offensive. If [a woman] enters [a male space], she is upsetting the male's order and his peace of mind. She is actually committing an act of aggression against him merely by being present where she should not be.
>
> The male's...logical response to an exhibitionistic assault...consists of pursuing the woman...pinching her if the occasion is propitious, eventually assaulting her verbally; all in the hope of convincing her to carry out her exhibitionistic propositioning to its implied end. (1975, 81–86)

The question is not whether there's a logic for any particular behavior within a culture—there's *always* a logic or why else would people behave that way?—but whether or not Claire can be persuaded by that logic. She may decide the Moslem view of sexuality is quite reasonable and not react the next time she is harassed in a bakery, or, more likely, decide not to frequent bakeries alone. Or she may decide that there is something fundamentally offensive about the fact that "public spaces...are by definition male spaces" and continue to find this behavior upsetting whenever she encounters it. For Claire, this would be an example of local behavior that is not going to be justified by any amount of cultural information and that will accordingly continue to be a cultural incident for her as long as she remains in Cairo.

The problem of unacceptable behaviors applies equally to Type II situations. Some of those same local behaviors you can't bring yourself to accept are, of course, behaviors the local people will expect *of you*. Needless to say, if you don't approve of these things when the locals do them, you're not about to do them yourself, even if that does mean committing a Type II incident. Many expats struggle mightily with this issue, for they know the more they conform to local norms, the more successful and effective they can be in their assignments. In some cases, they don't realize why they can't behave in a certain way, and they blame themselves for what they perceive as personal inadequacy. This dilemma is especially acute in organizations that value and strongly encourage their members to be as culturally sensitive as possible.

In some of these dilemmas, there's a perfectly honorable solution. You can explain to the local people that, even though you know what's expected of you, what's normally done in such and such a situation, for "personal reasons" you are unable to comply. This allows you to demonstrate that you are a culturally sensitive sort—you're not behaving inappropriately because you don't know any better—and at the same time to avoid having to engage in the behavior that offends you. Moreover, it shifts the blame from the host culture to you (personal reasons). The local people can easily identify with the concept of personal reasons—we've all had them in one instance or another—and forgive you for them.

93

In the Final Analysis

In the end, expats should not hesitate to draw the line when it comes to certain local behaviors, to admit that there will be things about the local culture that they will never be able to accept. While they should be careful not to consign behaviors to the unacceptable category prematurely, if they have truly understood why the local people behave as they do in a given situation and still cannot bring themselves to accept that behavior, then so be it. Expats should never try to force themselves to accept behaviors that violate their fundamental values; cultural effectiveness should not—and ultimately cannot—be purchased at the expense of one's self-respect. Expats must at times strive to transcend their cultural conditioning, but they must also beware of trying to alter their personalities. If they genuinely respect the local culture, they must permit themselves to be appalled by it. "When you come across an alien culture," one observer has noted, "you must not automatically respect it. You must sometimes pay it the compliment of hating it" (Mantel 1987, 26).

The message of this book is not that you must uncritically embrace all local behavior no matter how strange or offensive but only that you should not reject behaviors *before* you have understood them. In other words, always try to understand before you judge, but once you *have* understood, you *must* judge. Otherwise, you risk compromising your own identity.

This is a tricky business, as many observers have remarked. "To live in India," the novelist Ruth Prawer Jhabvala has observed,

> and be at peace, one must to a very considerable extent
> become Indian and adopt Indian attitudes, habits, beliefs,
> assume, if possible, an Indian personality. But how is this
> possible? And even if it were possible—without cheating
> oneself—would it be desirable? Should one try to become
> something other than what one is? (1987, 21)

T. E. Lawrence (of Arabia), culture-crosser extraordinaire, disappeared into Bedouin culture, the better, he thought, to achieve his mission. And achieve it he did, but at a cost he later came to question. "In my case," he wrote,

> the efforts for three years to live in the dress of Arabs, and
> to imitate their mental foundation, quitted me of my En-
> glish self and let me look at the West and its conventions
> with new eyes. They destroyed it all for me. At the same
> time I could not sincerely take on the Arab skin; it was an
> affectation only. Easily was a man made an infidel, but
> hardly might he be converted to another faith.... Sometimes
> these selves would converse in the void; and then madness
> was very near, as I believe it would be near the man who
> could see things through the veils at once of two customs,
> two educations, two environments. (1939, 30)

Becoming culturally effective does not mean becoming a local; it means trying to see the world the way the locals do and trying to imagine how they see you. If you can do that, you will have done all that's necessary to function effectively overseas. You will still encounter cultural incidents, though far fewer than someone who has not made this effort, but you will have earned the right to be offended. "The art of travel," Freya Stark wrote, "and perhaps of life, is to know when to give way and when not to" (1988, 183). So too the art of crossing cultures.

6

Language Lessons

When the tower of Babel fell
It caused a lot of unnecessary Hell.
Personal rapport
Became a complicated bore
And a lot more difficult than it had been before,
When the tower of Babel fell.

—Noel Coward
Collected Lyrics

One of the greatest allies the expat has in the quest to become culturally adept is the ability to speak the local language. Language learning is not one of the steps in our model of cultural effectiveness—it is not an essential skill for crossing cultures—but all other things being equal, it can be a tremendous asset. Speaking the language doesn't guarantee you will be effective abroad—it's as easy to be a bilingual boor as a monolingual one—any more than not speaking it guarantees you won't. But of all the variables that influence the process of crossing cultures, speaking the local language can make the most difference, which is how it comes to have its own brief chapter in this book.

Practically Speaking

Speaking the local language works wonders on what we've called country shock, that series of adjustments to the country, the community, and the job described in chapter 1. Knowing the language to even a limited degree doesn't mean you won't have the same bewildering number of things to learn about and get used to in the new country, but imagine how much easier it will be to learn them if you can talk to and understand the local people. Nor should we forget that both the pace and stress of country shock directly affect how well and quickly you will adjust to the culture; anything that abets the former abets the latter.

Knowing the language can also have a direct impact on preventing cultural incidents. Just by virtue of understanding what's being said around you, you can better understand cross-cultural encounters. If you can speak the language, you can question a much broader range of people about the culture, often getting more valuable information than you do from the educated elites you must rely on if you don't know the language. Needless to say, whatever helps prevent cultural incidents, whether Type I or Type II, virtually guarantees greater effectiveness both on and off the job.

Because language is one of the principle means through which you can manipulate and control your environment and thereby enjoy a sense of well-being and security, the lack of language, not surprisingly, is one of the main reasons for feeling so helpless and vulnerable during the first few months abroad. There is the ever-present possibility that you may suddenly find yourself in situations where you can't make yourself understood, where, for want of being able to express your needs, you leave the situation with those needs unmet. Who hasn't had the experience of going to a shop and leaving without getting what you wanted for lack of being able to describe it or spot it on the shelf? And how much more serious is the issue if it is medicine you need, if you're lost, or if there's been an accident and you need help?

Invidious Comparisons

It's not much fun, as Edward Gibbon recalled in his *Memoirs*.

> *When I was thus suddenly cast on foreign land I found my-self deprived of the use of speech and hearing; and, during some weeks, incapable not only of enjoying the pleasures of conversation, but even of asking or answering a question in the common intercourse of life.... From a man I was again degraded to the dependence of a schoolboy...and helpless and awkward as I have ever been. My condition seemed as destitute of hope as it was devoid of pleasure.* (Massingham and Massingham 1984, 15)

99

Clearly, feeling like a schoolboy does little to boost an expat's self-esteem and self-confidence, two more casualties of being unable to speak the local language. Average, articulate adults, capable in so many other ways, who are suddenly transformed into virtual mutes, who can only nod and smile foolishly when addressed by well-intentioned, monolingual locals, find the experience demeaning. For all their competence, they feel—and in a sense, are—inferior to the three-year-old neighbor child who may still wet his pants but at least knows how to count to ten. It's an open question who might fare better in a tight spot.

In *Living Poor*, his classic book about the Peace Corps, Moritz Thomsen captures the feeling exactly:

> *On this trip to Machala...I made my first close emotional contact with a national...a man of about forty with a foxy little black moustache and quick, black buttonhole eyes. There was no place for him to sit on the bus, so he squatted in the aisle, put his head in my lap, and quietly passed out.... He*

awoke suddenly, after one particularly spectacular bump...and found himself staring into the face of a gringo.

He was thunderstruck...it was obvious he loved gringos. He began to pat my head. And he began to talk. He talked a torrent of Spanish, but I could scarcely understand perfect Castilian...let alone the coastal patois...well mixed with sleep and alcohol. I couldn't understand a word he said, not one single word, and I had to sit there...smiling like a dummy, surreptitiously wiping off the flecks of spit that he enthusiastically directed at my face. The other passengers were watching me with expressions of increasing pity as it dawned on them, one by one, that the gringo was a half-wit. My friend finally realized it too and gazed at me with a baffled look on his face.... To tell you the truth, for about three hours on that wild plunge to the coastal tropics, this was exactly how I saw myself. (1989a, 23–24)

Reeling from incidents such as these, you will want to run away, illustrating another unfortunate consequence of not knowing the language: the necessity, or at least the tendency, to spend more and more time with your compatriots in the foreign colony. Who likes to be reminded of their ineptitude or to be compared unfavorably to a three-year-old? Ego bruised, your pride under siege, you crave the reassurance of the foreign community where you can once again be the master of the situation. There's no harm done, of course, as long as you can sally forth once your wounds have healed, but that's just it: it's very tempting not to. And then the entire dynamic, as noted in chapter 3, becomes self-sustaining; not speaking the language, insecure, you retreat into the expatriate subculture where—is it any surprise?—your command of the local language does not notably improve.

Deeper Meanings

Another dividend of knowing the language is the insight it offers into the culture; you can't learn the language of a people without also learning the "grammar" and "vocabulary" of their worldview. The student of Arabic, for example, learns that "God willing" (*N'sha'llah*) is automatically added to any statement about the future (just as "thanks be to God" accompanies any reference to fortunate events of the past), that many common given names—Abdullah, Abdelsalam, Abdelwahid—translate as slave *(abd)* of God, appreciating, as a consequence, the essential fatalism of Arab culture. Similarly, the student of Nepali, struggling to sort out the myriad nouns for family members—there are four words for uncle, denoting whether the man in question is the brother of one's father or mother and whether he is older or younger than said parent—readily appreciates the importance of the family in Nepali society and may even intuit the relative insignificance of the individual. Language is not simply how people speak; it is who they are.

On a deeper level, if you can't communicate your ideas and opinions to people, how can they know who you are? And if you can't understand others, how can you know them? You can still interact with these people—they may know a little of your language and you a little of theirs—and relate in other ways, but these relationships must necessarily be superficial. Not truly knowing others, not feeling you are known by them, you feel alone and isolated. "What I find trying in a country which you do not understand and where you cannot speak," Freya Stark has observed, "is that you can never be *yourself*. You are English, or Christian, or Protestant, or anything but your individual *you*..." (1988, 4).

There is another kind of isolation many expats also feel. Language is the primary means of self-expression; when we don't have language, the self does not get expressed. When the self can no longer be expressed, does it still exist? There is a loneliness expats feel that has nothing to do with being away from family and friends or not having friends in the new country; they feel estranged from themselves. "Because I speak no Portuguese," Moritz Thomsen wrote of a trip through Brazil, "and have chosen to move through those parts of [Rio de Janeiro] where tourists do not go, I find after a few days of not speaking that I have begun to doubt my own existence" (1989b, 3).

Perhaps the most compelling reason to learn the language of another land is the largely symbolic significance of the act of communication. Implicit in that act, after all, is the acknowledgment of the humanity and worth of the other person, especially when one is speaking in a language other than one's own. Anyone who has ever learned another language knows the effort involved and appreciates it, therefore, when a foreigner has gone to the trouble to learn their language. In the end, what matters is not what we say when we speak Russian or Chinese, but what the effort to speak Russian or Chinese says about us. "Learning a native language," Charles Allen has observed, "was perhaps the best thing that ever happened to people who went out to India, and those who failed to do so remained forever at a distance from the land and its people" (1984, 75).

This is all well and good, you may be saying, but I'm only here for two years and it will take me that long just to achieve basic competence, and that would only be if I had the time for language classes, which I don't. This is certainly a valid point, but it overlooks the fact that you can begin to enjoy most of the benefits of speaking the local language long before you become proficient, almost immediately in fact. You start to feel less vulnerable, for example, as soon as you master a few basic phrases and make your first purchase or the first time you successfully ask for and understand directions. You start learning about the culture as soon as you begin your language study, and you don't have to be fluent for people to appreciate the effort you're making to talk to them (especially if your native tongue is one of the "world" languages, such as English, Spanish or French). And you can always start studying the language before you arrive overseas. In any event, when considering whether or not to study the language, remember that proficiency is neither the only nor the most important criterion.

7

The Payoff

Father, Mother, and Me,
Sister and Auntie say
All the people like us are We,
And everyone else is They.
And They live over the sea
While we live over the way,
But—would you believe it?—They look upon We
As only a sort of They!

We eat pork and beef
With cow-horn-handled knives.
They who gobble Their rice off a leaf
Are horrified out of Their lives;
While They who live up a tree,
Feast on grubs and clay,
(Isn't it scandalous?) look upon We
As a simply disgusting They!

We eat kitcheny food.
We have doors that latch.
They drink milk and blood
Under an open thatch. We have doctors to fee.

They have wizards to pay.
And (impudent heathen!) They look upon We
As a quite impossible They!

All good people agree,
And all good people say,
All nice people, like us, are We
And everyone else is They:
But if you cross over the sea,
Instead of over the way,
You may end by (think of it!) looking on We
As only a sort of They!

—Rudyard Kipling
"We and They"

106

Cultural effectiveness comes at the cost of vigilance and sustained effort. It requires that you keep a close watch over how you spend your time, that you resist the natural temptation to seek out the familiar and the comfortable, that you train yourself to monitor your emotional states, and, finally, that you try not to judge the local people before you have understood them. If all this sounds a tad superhuman—and parts of it do seem to fly in the face of human nature—try to remember that there isn't any real alternative. If you're going to be truly successful in an overseas assignment, then you have to become culturally effective. Many expats do not, of course, settling for being somewhat or occasionally or slightly effective—as if that cost was somehow less dear.

So your task may be daunting, but as with any challenge worth taking up, the rewards are commensurate with the effort. Just what those rewards are is the subject of this final chapter.

Getting the Job Done

The most obvious reward for being culturally effective is that it greatly increases your chances of accomplishing whatever objectives you had in going abroad, both for yourself and for your organization. No one likes to fail, especially not in an undertaking of this magnitude, in which you invest months and years of your time and energy (and that of your family). Your company or organization doesn't want you to fail either, of course, having also invested considerably in your assignment.

Successful expats add great value to their organizations, not only in discharging their responsibilities and completing their mission overseas, but also in the form of greatly enhanced skills and knowledge the company can use, whether at headquarters or in other locations. In addition, successful expats are a great advertisement for global companies having trouble recruiting for overseas assignments (just as early returnees are the worst kind of publicity). In a recent survey of 264 global corporations, two-thirds of the respondents cited finding qualified candidates as the most critical challenge to their international operations (Windham 1999, 24).

Another advantage of being culturally aware is that the better you understand the local culture, the harder it is for the locals to hide behind it. The Filipino marketing director who doesn't want the bother of developing a new advertising campaign can always find a cultural explanation for why the suggested new approach won't work. And who are you, even if you suspect a trick, to call the Filipino's bluff? If you have adapted, however, if you know the culture and therefore can see the director's game, you can make short work of it. Indeed, if the marketing director is perceptive or knows you well, she won't waste her time trying to fool you in the first place.

In this context it is interesting to note that the Japanese, unlike most peoples, do not always appreciate it when a foreigner speaks their language well. Part of the reason for this is that fluency in the language allows the foreigner to penetrate the public persona the Japanese so carefully cultivate and come to know the individual personality beneath. This in turn cancels the natural advantage the notoriously formal Japanese have in dealing with outsiders, particularly Westerners, who wear their thoughts and feelings on their sleeves. It is possible that the Japanese record of success in business is as much a function of their infamous inscrutability as it is their way with lasers and microchips.

A related advantage here is that if it is known that you know the culture, then any changes or improvements you need or want to make in local operations will be taken much more seriously by the indigenous workforce. Expats and their bosses back home are always looking for ways to add value and improve performance. If local employees know you understand the local reality and culture, they will be much more likely to give your schemes a fair trial. If they think you don't, they'll have little faith in your decisions and will spend most of their time trying to quietly distance themselves as much as possible from the imminent failure of the latest best practice.

Put yourself in the shoes of the locals. You're the head of public relations or new product development in New York or London. You get a new boss, from Germany, let's say, who's never lived in your country, speaks very ungrammatical English, makes cultural mistakes right and left, and has never quite got the hang of pronouncing your name. And she proposes a bold new scheme. What would *your* reaction be?

Being Yourself and Distinguishing the Individual from the Culture

Another consequence of being culturally effective is the sense of security it allows you to feel. Ignorance is the breeding ground of fear and anxiety. Not knowing what the locals will do or how they will react to what you do next produces a constant tension and feeling of unease. You can never be altogether confident or comfortable, never free of the almost palpable suspicion that what you don't know can indeed hurt you.

On a related note, the process of coming to know the local culture frees you to relax and be yourself again. Not knowing which of your behaviors may be culturally acceptable and which may not, and knowing, furthermore, that your behavior reflects not only on you but also on your organization, you may err on the side of caution in your interactions with the local people, tiptoeing your way through intercultural situations in a state of semiparalysis. You closely monitor your behavior and your speech, alert to signs that anything you've done might have caused offense. It's the "walking-on-eggshells" syndrome, and it's exhausting. Indeed, the strain prompts many expats to limit discretionary contact with the local people so they can recover between outings.

109

Once you begin to understand the culture, however, and learn what is appropriate and what is not, you can release your grip on your instincts and let your personality loose. In a word, you can relax. The relief you feel is enormous, and the local people, not incidentally, find it much easier to be with you.

The locals undergo a similar metamorphosis once you begin to understand their culture: that is, they too become themselves. They have been themselves all along, of course, but not to you. Until you know the local culture reasonably well, you can never be sure, in your dealings with individuals, which behaviors of theirs are mandated by the culture and which are peculiar to them as individuals. If a colleague is hurt when you fail to remember her birthday, is it because the culture sets great store by birthdays and personal relationships in general (and you'd better not forget those of your other colleagues either) or is it merely that Rosita is particularly sensitive on this subject—a useful piece of information if it's true? When you shout at a merchant who won't take back a defective lamp, are you being boorish by reacting to an accepted cultural practice or is the man in fact a cheat, someone the locals would also shout at and whom you'd be foolish to indulge? Until you know the culture, you can never be sure.

But once you do, your experience abroad is radically transformed. You can now separate the individual from his or her culture or, more accurately, distinguish individuals within the culture. Suddenly, everyone has a distinctive personality; you like— or, rather, you are free to like—certain people and not others. And you understand that you must treat Horst in one manner and Klaus in another. You can begin to have personal relationships with people or have more, or sometimes less, confidence in those relationships you may already have established. And as the people you know are revealed more clearly to you, you in turn are comfortable in revealing more of yourself to them.

Seeing the World Anew

Another great boon of becoming culturally effective is the ability to see the world from a new perspective. As you learn about the local culture, and especially as you learn the beliefs and values behind various local norms, you begin to see the world from that point of view. This doesn't mean you abandon your own viewpoint (though you may make some adjustments) but only that you are now able to see the same behaviors and attitudes from more than one perspective. You begin to understand that behavior that makes no sense to you might make perfect sense to others. And vice versa. You're not so quick to judge anymore, or at least to judge quite so harshly. You begin to think more seriously about, even to tolerate, opinions and actions you would have dismissed before.

You give the benefit of the doubt where previously you would have had no doubt whatsoever. You add to who you are. Aldous Huxley wrote,

> *So the journey is over and I am back again where I started, richer by much experience and poorer by many exploded convictions, many perished certainties. For convictions and certainties are too often the concomitants of ignorance. Those who like to feel they are always right and who attach a high importance to their own opinions should stay at home. When one is travelling, convictions are mislaid as easily as spectacles; but unlike spectacles, they are not easily replaced.* (1985, 206–07)

The ability to see situations, problems, practices—the way we do things—from multiple perspectives, from the way *other people* see things, is a tremendous benefit to you and to your company when you go back home. Whatever the question or circumstances, you can always see alternatives to the standard response. Thinking outside the box, changing paradigms, reinventing the organization—overseas, you do it every day.

111

It is not only the specific ways expats change that are of such benefit to them, but also the realization that they are *capable* of changing in such significant ways. If people know they can change, that they're survivors, then the world becomes a much less formidable place. Expats who bounce back again and again from the challenges and frustrations of living overseas can be forgiven for thinking they can handle whatever life throws at them.

Discovering Your Own Culture

Another benefit of learning about a foreign culture is that in the process we learn a great deal about our own. At home we are rarely prompted to reflect on our cultural selves; we are too busy manifesting our behavior to examine it, and even if we were thus inclined, what would we use as our vantage point? Once we encounter another frame of reference, however, we begin to see what we never could before. When we notice the unusual behavior of a foreigner, we are at that moment noticing our own behavior as well. We only notice a difference (something unusual) in reference to a norm or standard (the usual) and that norm we refer to is invariably our own behavior. Thus it is that through daily contact with the customs and habits of people from a foreign culture, our attention is repeatedly focused on our own customs and habits, that in encountering another culture, we simultaneously and for the first time encounter our own.

It is only a slight exaggeration to say that the average expatriate, even the average tourist, returns from a stay abroad knowing more about his or her own country than about the one just visited. As T. S. Eliot wrote in a famous passage in *Four Quartets,*

> We shall not cease from exploration,
> And the end of all our exploring
> Will be to arrive where we started
> And know the place for the first time. (1962, 145)

Lawrence Durrell felt the same: "Journeys," he writes, "lead us not only outwards in space, but inwards as well. Travel can be one of the most rewarding forms of introspection" (1957, 15).

It would be difficult to exaggerate the significance of this inward journey. Living abroad presents us with a unique opportunity for self-discovery and, thereby, for self-improvement. Each of us has in effect two personalities: an individual one that is the product of the particular circumstances of our lives and that accounts for how we are different from those around us, and a cultural one that is the product of cultural conditioning and accounts for how we are the same as everyone around us. And each of these personalities (or

aspects of our personalities) is the source of wholesome and un-
wholesome behavior. When we are made aware of these behaviors,
we can try to cultivate the former and eradicate the latter.

But while we can come to know and change our individual
selves without leaving our own culture (through interacting with
other individuals), we cannot come to know our cultural selves
without the benefit of an equivalent vantage point. Thus it is that
until we go abroad or otherwise spend time with foreigners, this
cultural self lies beyond our awareness, directing and influencing
our behavior in ways we can only guess at. "Those who go abroad,"
Edmond Taylor writes, "step out of their own culture and begin
to...discover how it influences personal life" (1964, xiii). While
we would no doubt approve of many of these influences if we were
aware of them, we might not approve of others and might want to
change them.

In going overseas and encountering local culture, we are able
see our own cultural personality in action. And only when we've
seen it can we decide whether or not we like it. "By broadening
his conception of the forces which make up and control his life,"
Edward Hall observes,

> the average person can never again be caught in the grip of
> patterned behavior of which he has no awareness. While it
> is true that culture binds human beings in many unknown
> ways, the restraint it exercises is the groove of habit and
> nothing more. Man did not evolve culture as a means of
> smothering himself but as a medium in which to move, live,
> breathe, and discover his own uniqueness. (1990, 187)

As one expat put it, much more succinctly, "I have a better idea of
how I tick" (Osland 1995, 154).

By far the greatest reward of becoming culturally effective is
the fate it saves us from. The alternative is to live and work among

people we don't understand and therefore can never entirely trust. It means living and working among people who repeatedly annoy and upset us, toward whom we become increasingly critical and negative, and compared with whom we feel increasingly superior. It means the artificial reality and forced friendships of life in the expatriate subculture. It is a prescription for the narrowing of our humanity, for our ability to be sympathetic and compassionate people.

In another context, the anthropologist Vincent Crapanzano has chronicled this phenomenon. If we substitute our own "withdrawing" for his "waiting," we have a picture of the true cost of turning away from the local culture.

114

> *In the very ordinary act of waiting, particularly of waiting in fear, men and women lose what John Keats called "negative capability," the capability of so negating their identity as to be imaginatively open to the complex and never very certain reality around them. Instead, they close off; they create a kind of psychological apartheid....* (1986, xxii)

You can only hope that when your sojourn is over and you are once again inclined to open yourself up to others, you will still know how.

Many expats won't need a list like this to persuade them they should adjust to the local culture; they'll do it simply because it's the right thing. Even so, it's nice to know the right thing has so much to recommend it.

Conclusion

This book has been quite critical of cultural incidents to make its point: if you aren't careful—if you don't *do something* about these incidents—you can easily turn against the local culture and compromise your effectiveness. Cultural incidents are a legitimate cause for concern.

At the same time, there is a great deal to be said in their defense. If you follow the advice offered in this book, then cultural incidents become the motivation for learning about the local culture instead of turning against it, and in the process for learning about your own culture and yourself. Moreover, dealing with these incidents forces you to practice greater self-awareness, which is always beneficial. In the final analysis, cultural incidents themselves aren't the problem; it's how you react to them. If you react constructively, you will derive great benefit.

It would be a mistake, meanwhile, to assume there is no urgency in this matter. The overseas experience profoundly transforms all who undergo it, whether they interact successfully with the local culture or not. Such is the impact of the experience, on so many levels—physical, intellectual, emotional—there is no possibility of a moderate, much less a neutral, reaction. You either open yourself up to the experience and are greatly enriched by it, or you turn away—and are greatly diminished.

Appendix: Eloquent Witness

Some of the most penetrating insights into the art of crossing cultures have come from travel writers and writers of what we might call expatriate fiction, novels that feature characters living outside their home culture and whose central theme is the experience of being foreign. E. M. Forster's *A Passage to India* is a classic of that genre.

Observation is a writer's stock in trade, so one might expect that writers would subject the overseas experience to close scrutiny. But it is the combination of penetrating observation and a way with words that makes so many of their insights indelible. Indeed, perhaps they're not any better observers than you or I are; maybe it's just that they describe what they see so well it seems that they must be. Or maybe it's just that they give what they see and experience more thought; it's a writer's job, after all, not just to record experience but to tell us what it means.

This book has relied repeatedly on such writers to make many of its points and hereby offers more selections for those of you who enjoy this sort of thing. They are arranged according to various topics covered in these pages.

On the various components of country shock:

The strain of living and thinking in a foreign land and half-understood language, the savage food, strange clothes, and still stranger ways, with the complete loss of privacy and quiet, and the impossibility of ever relaxing your watchful imitation of the others for months on end, provide such an added stress to the ordinary difficulties of dealing with the Bedu, the climate, and the Turks, that this road should not be chosen without serious thought.
　　　　　　　　　　　　　　—T. E. Lawrence (of Arabia)

It is so very HOT I do not know how to write it large enough.
　　　　　　　　　　　　　　—Emily Eden
　　　　　　　　　　　　　　Up the Country

I've been in Ceylon a month and nearly sweated myself into a shadow.
　　　　　　　　　　　　　　—D. H. Lawrence
　　　　　　　　　　　　　　Letters

As she made up her face, cursing the sweat that clogged the powder, she was sick for London, coolly making up for a dance in the evening, or for the ballet, or for a concert. Civilization is only possible in a temperate zone.
　　　　　　　　　　　　　　—Anthony Burgess
　　　　　　　　　　　　　　Time for A Tiger

When calculating our chances of obtaining health and pleasure from a tour abroad, we must think of the nervous irritation involved in waiting hours past our usual meal-times, of never being sure of sleep at night—suspecting, as we must, that just as we have dined off fellow-creatures, smaller fellow-creatures may sup off us!

—Rev. E. J. Hardy
Manners Makyth Man

'I've been fine lately,' said a junior officer, holding his end up, as it were. 'Knock on wood. I've had some severe—I mean, really bad times. But I figured it out. What I usually do is have yogurt. I drink tons of the stuff. I figure the bacteria in yogurt keeps down the bacteria in lousy food. Kind of an equalizing thing.'

There was another man. He looked pale, but he said he was bearing up. Kind of a bowel thing. Up all night. Cramps. Delhi belly. Food goes right through you. He said, 'I had it in spades. Bacillary. Ever have bacillary? No? It knocked me flat. For six days I couldn't do a thing. Running back and forth, practically living in the john.'

Each time the subject came up, I wanted to take the speaker by his hand-loomed shirt, and, shaking him, say, 'Now listen to me! There is absolutely nothing wrong with your bowels!'

—Paul Theroux
The Great Railway Bazaar

119

But what is there to like? Scabby children, spitting pot-bellied shopkeepers, terrorists, burglars, scorpions, those blasted flying-beetles. And the noise of the radios and the eternal shouting. Are they deaf or something? Where is this glamorous East they talk about? It's just a horrible sweating travesty of Europe.

—Anthony Burgess
Time For A Tiger

Other losses, although not at first felt, tell heavily after a period: these are the want of room, of seclusion, of rest; the jading feeling of constant hurry; the privation of small luxuries, the loss of domestic society, and even of music and the other pleasures of imagination.

—Charles Darwin
The Voyage of the Beagle

The people are not handsome, have no idea of friendly society. There is no ice or cold water, no baths or colleges, no candles, no torches, not a single candlestick.

—Babur
The Mogul Conqueror of India

On culture shock; the strange things the locals do.

I subsequently learnt that although the Fans will eat their fellow friendly tribesfolk, yet they like to keep a little something belonging to them as a memento. This touching trait in their character I learnt from Wiki; and though it's to their credit, under the circumstances, still it's an unpleasant practice when they hang the remains in the bedroom you occupy.

—Mary Kingsley
Travels in West Africa

If you want to know what it is to feel the 'correct' social world fizzle to nothing you should come to Australia. It is a weird place. In the established sense, it is socially nil. Happy-go-lucky, don't-you-bother, we're-in-Australia. But also there seems to be no inside life of any sort: just a long lapse and drift. A rather fascinating indifference, a physical indifference to what we call soul or spirit. It's really a weird show....

A strange effect it has on one. Often I hate it like poison, then again it fascinates me, and the spell of its indifference gets me.

—D. H. Lawrence
The Letters of D. H. Lawrence

The first month or two in class I was always saying, 'Look at me when I talk to you,' and the [Navajo] kids simply wouldn't do it. They would always look at their hands, or the blackboard, or anywhere except looking me in the face. And finally one of the other teachers told me it was a cultural thing. They should warn us about things like that. Odd things. It makes the children seem evasive, deceptive.

—Tony Hillerman
The Skinwalkers

121

Each car we passed raised a cheer from my fellow passengers. I closed my eyes as, tires screeching, we took a blind corner, swerving across into the right-hand lane. This too raised a cheer. Did death mean nothing to them? They had slipped beyond my imaginative reach. The driver, wedged between the angle of the door and the seat, could hardly be bothered to glance at the road ahead. Frequently he would remove both his hands from the steering wheel, the better to emphasize some point to the fat lady sitting next to him, with whom he was deep in conversation. Out of the corner of my eye I caught a fleeting glimpse of a chicken plummeting past the window. A terrific commotion ensued. We stopped, and a search party was organized. The chicken was found alive, but stunned, and restored to its place on the roof rack.

—Shiva Naipaul
North of South

On culture shock; the strange things *we* do:

Washing my face in the morning caused much speculation at the village of Las Minas; a superior tradesman closely cross-questioned me about so singular a practice.

—Charles Darwin
The Voyage of the Beagle

But our English trick of shaking hands, they look upon as the most hoity toity impudent custom in the world and cannot reconcile it with the vestal demeanor of the English Ladies.

—Catherine Wilmot
An Irish Peer on the Continent

[The women of the harem] pitied us European women heartily, that we had to go about travelling, and appearing in the streets without being properly taken care of—that is, watched. They think us strangely neglected in being left so free, and boast of [how closely they are watched] as a token of the value in which they are held.

—Harriet Martineau
Eastern Life

The first mosquitoes of the year appeared at Nomo Khantara and as I killed one on my arm the lama sadly reproved me. To show me how to act in such circumstances he took a sand-louse that was marching on to my rug and, handling it gently, deposited it outside the tent.

—Ella Maillart
Forbidden Journey

The fact was that Victor Crabbe, after a mere six months in the Federation, had reached that position common among veteran expatriates—he saw that a white skin was an abnormality, and that the white man's ways were fundamentally eccentric.

—Anthony Burgess
Time For A Tiger

But you who are wise must know that different Nations have different Conceptions of things and you will therefore not take it amiss if our Ideas of this kind of Education happen not to be the same as yours. We have had some Experience of it. Several of our Young People were formerly brought up at the Colleges of the Northern Provinces: they were instructed in all your Sciences; but when they came back to us they were bad Runners, ignorant of every means of living in the woods...neither fit for Hunters, Warriors, nor Counsellors, they were totally good for nothing.

We are, however, not the less obliged by your kind Offer, though we decline accepting it; and to show our grateful Sense of it, if the Gentlemen of Virginia will send us a Dozen of their Sons, we will take Care of their Education, instruct them in all we know, and make Men of them.

—Response of the Indians of the Six Nations
to a suggestion that they send boys to an
American college in Pennsylvania (1744)

Turning against the local culture:

You are absolutely unlike the others, I assure you. You will never be rude to my people.
I'm told we all get rude after a year.

—E. M. Forster
A Passage to India

Do you like India? Mrs. Bristow asked me.
Oh, yes, I think it's marvelous.
And what do you think of the people?
I like them very much and think them most interesting.
Oh, aren't you a fibber. What was it you said the other day
about 'awful Anglo-Indian' chatter?'
But I thought you were speaking of the Indians just now,
not the Anglo-Indians.
The Indians! I never think of them.
Well, you said 'the people,' you know.
I meant us people, stupid!
I see. Well now, let's start again.

—J. R. Ackerly
Hindoo Holiday

124

It was not difficult for me to work up a rage at this moment.
All of a sudden I felt that revulsion against an alien way of
life that anyone who travels in remote places feels from
time to time. I longed for clean clothes, the company of
people who meant what they said, and did it.

—Eric Newby
A Short Walk in the Hindu Kush

'Very well. I'll go. And I shan't be sorry either. I haven't had
a decent meal since I came here and I've done a thing I
never thought I should have to do in my life, I've drunk my
coffee without sugar and when I've been lucky enough to
get a little piece of black bread I've had to eat it without
butter. Mrs. Harrington will never believe me when I tell her
what I've gone through.

—Somerset Maugham
"Mr. Harrington's Washing"

I never told you, but there was a time—my second month in India last year—when if someone had offered me a passage home I'd have accepted like a shot. Goodness knows I loved being with you. But during that second month I had what I can only describe as a permanent sinking heart. I hated everything, hated it because I was afraid of it. It was all so alien.

—Paul Scott
The Day of the Scorpion

On life in the expatriate subculture:

Arab Town, at any hour of the day or night, was a fascinating place to us, and it was astonishing to discover how ignorant the English colony were about it, and how uninterested. Many of them had never been there at all. Although it was only a few streets away, they were as vague about it as Londoners are about Limehouse. They had an idea that it smelled and crawled with bugs, and that was enough for them, though they showed a tolerance of my interest, remarking that every chap has his own game; I was one of those writing johnnies, so of course I had to nose around a bit collecting local colour; jolly interesting too for a chap who was interested in that sort of thing; they would read all about it in my book when that came out; meanwhile, snooker and whisky-soda for them.

—Evelyn Waugh
Labels

125

There are children, frail and moribund, who live inside plastic bubbles; their immune systems have not developed, and so they have to be protected from the outside world, their air specially filtered, and their nourishment passed to them through special ducts, by gloved and sterile hands. Profes-

sional expatriates live like that.... They carry about with them the plastic bubble of their own culture, and nothing touches them until it has been filtered through the protective membrane of prejudice, the life-support system that forms their invisible excess baggage when they move on, from one contract to the next, to another country and another set of complaints.

—Hilary Mantel
"Last Morning in Al Hamra"
Spectator 24 January 1987

You know what you are sent abroad for. It is of much more consequence to know the Mores multorum hominum *than the* Urbes. *Pray continue this judicious conduct wherever you go, especially at Paris, where instead of thirty you will find above three hundred English herding together, and conversing with no one French body.*

The life of les Milords Anglais *is regularly, or if you will, irregularly this. As soon as they rise, which is very late, they breakfast together to the utter loss of two good morning hours. Then they go by coachfuls to the Palais, the Invalides, and Notre-Dame; from thence to the English coffee-house, where they make up their tavern party for dinner. From dinner, where they drink, they adjourn in clusters to the play, where they crowd up the stage, drest up in very fine clothes, very ill made by a Scotch or Irish tailor.... Those who do not speak French before they go are sure to learn none there. Thus, they return home more petulant, but not more informed, than when they left it; and show, as they think, their improvement, by affectedly both speaking and dressing in broken French.*

—Lord Chesterfield
Letters

No islands could seemingly be more different, one from the other. But to the Englishman superficially they will seem the same. The English carry their own lives with them. They make no attempt to assimilate into the character of the countries they occupy.... An Englishman arriving at an English-governed community knows precisely what is awaiting him. He will present his letters of introduction, and immediately he will be received into the life of the community. He becomes a part of whatever fun is going.

—Alec Waugh
Hot Countries

Advice on adjusting to a foreign culture:

The ideal traveller, in fact, is not a man who goes out to teach, but a man who goes out to learn. He is a person who, in his most censorious moments, even as he wickedly observes the Italians juggling with spaghetti or listens to the tiresome yodelling of the Swiss, can look at himself and realize that he is equally funny—that his favorite dish is fish and chips, that his grey trousers and sports coat can make him seem inexpressibly comic to a Spaniard or an Arab.

—Hugh and Pauline Massingham
The Englishman Abroad

If I had to write a decalogue for journeys, eight out of ten virtues should be moral, and I should put first of all a temper as serene at the end as at the beginning of the day. Then would come the capacity to accept values and to judge by standards other than our own...[and] a leisurely and uncensorious mind.

—Freya Stark
A Winter in Arabia

127

A Russian invariably takes off his hat whenever he enters beneath a roof, be it palace, cottage, or hovel; the reason for which is that in every apartment of every Russian house there hangs in one corner of it, just below the ceiling, a picture of the Virgin. To omit conforming to this usage, and paying respect to the penates of the dwelling, will not be either wise or well-bred, for it may give offence; a man has no business to travel in foreign countries who cannot make up his mind to conform to their customs.

—John Murray
*Murray's Handbook
for Northern Europe*

In the meantime, we've got to live here. We've got to try and make some sort of life in this country. It's no good fighting against it all the time. You've got to accept that this isn't London, that the climate's equatorial, that there aren't concerts and theatres and ballets. But there are other things. The people themselves, the little drinking shops, the incredible mixture of religions and cultures and languages. That's what we're here for—to absorb the country. Or be absorbed by it, he said to himself.

—Anthony Burgess
The Enemy in the Blanket

On being from two cultures:

I can hardly explain to you the queer feeling of living, as I do, in two places at once. One world containing books, England, and all the people with whom I can exchange an idea; the other is all that I actually see and hear and speak to. The separation is as complete as between the things in a picture and the things in a room. The puzzle is that both move and act, and I must say my say as one of each. The result is that one world at least must think me crazy. I am just now in a sad mess. A drover, who has grown rich with cattle dealing, wanted me to go and teach his daughter. As the man is a widower I astonished this world when I accepted the proposal, and still more because I asked too high a price a year. Now that I have begun, the same people can't conceive why I don't go on and marry the man at once, which they imagine must have been my original intention.

—Mary Taylor
quoted in H. Bolitho and J. Mulgan
The Emigrants: Early Travellers to the Antipodes

Sitting with Hari and Aunt Shalini this time I saw how unreal my life had become because there didn't seem to be any kind of future in front of me that I wanted and could have. Why? Holding one hand out, groping, and the other out backwards, linked to the security of what was known and expected. Straining like that. Pretending that the ground between was occupied, when all the time it wasn't.

—Paul Scott
The Jewel in the Crown

'I went a little farther,' he said. 'Then still a little farther— till I had gone so far that I don't know how I'll ever get back.'

—Joseph Conrad
"Heart of Darkness"

It's not necessary to like everything:

There is a special problem of adjustment for the sort of people who come today, who tend to be liberal in outlook and have been educated to be sensitive and receptive to other cul-

129

tures. But it is not always easy to be sensitive and receptive to India: there comes a point where you have to close up in order to protect yourself. The place is very strong and often proves too strong for European nerves.

—Ruth Prawer Jhabvala
Out of India

There were many things he found offensive but which he learned to accept because they were necessary, and equally a number of things that were unacceptable because they were offensive without being necessary. The worst of these was noise. Hour by hour and day after day columns of vans and cars, loudspeakers blaring, circled the estate laying a cordon of noise from which there was no escape.... Most Japanese had become resigned to this violation of their peace and assured Boon that he would soon get used to it, but he didn't.

—John David Morley
Pictures from the Water Trade

On language:

It's a funny thing; the French call it a couteau, *the Germans call it a* Messer, *but we call it a knife, which is after all what it really is.*

—Richard Jenkyns
The Victorians and Ancient Greece

They spell it Vinci and pronounce it Vinchy. Foreigners always spell better than they pronounce.

—Mark Twain

My head, still giddy from the motion of the ship, is confused by the multiplicity of novel objects: the dress of the people, the projecting roofs and balconies of the houses, the filth of the streets, so strange and so disgusting to an Englishman. But what is most strange is to hear a language which conveys to me only the melancholy reflection that I am in a land of strangers.

—Robert Southey
Letters

Sometime in 1906 I was walking in the heat of the day through the Bazaars. As I passed an Arab Cafe, in no hostility to my straw hat but desiring to shine before his friends, a fellow called out in Arabic, 'God curse your father, O Englishman.' I was young then and quicker tempered, and could not refrain from answering in his own language that I would also curse his father if he were in a position to inform me which of his mother's two and ninety admirers his father had been. I heard footsteps behind me, and slightly picked up the pace, angry with myself for committing the sin Lord Cromer would not pardon—a row with Egyptians. In a few seconds I felt a hand on each arm. 'My brother,' said the original humorist, 'return and drink with us coffee and smoke (in Arabic one speaks of 'drinking' smoke). I did not think that your worship knew Arabic, still less the correct Arabic abuse, and we would fain benefit further by your important thoughts.'

—Ronald Storrs
Orientations

We travelled in a big truck through the nation of France, on our way to Belgium, and every time we passed through a little town, we'd see these signs—"Boulangerie," "Patisserie," and "Rue" this and "Rue" that and rue the day you came here young man. When we got to our hundred and eightieth French village, I screamed at the top of my lungs: "The joke is over! English, please!" I couldn't believe a whole country couldn't speak English. One third of a nation, all right, but not a whole country.

—Mel Brooks
in Kenneth Tynan's *Show People*

Living overseas puts your own culture in perspective:

Familiarity blunts astonishment. Fishes do not marvel at water; they are too busy swimming in it. It is the same with us. We take our Western civilization for granted and find nothing intrinsically odd or incongruous in it. Before we can realize the strangeness of our surroundings, we must deliberately stop and think. But [overseas] moments come when that strangeness is fairly forced upon our notice, moments when an anomaly, a contradiction, an immense incongruity is suddenly illumined by a light so glaring that we cannot fail to see it.

—Aldous Huxley
Jesting Pilate

I always turn up the last page or two of a book of travels, even if I've only read bits of the book itself. When the traveller we've followed through remote scenes takes his latchkey from his pocket and runs up his own front steps, I want to know what is his view of his native land, how do things at home look to him through those eyes which have seen such events and adventures as he has recounted? Does the dingy snugness of England irk or gladden him, when he lands at Dover after months in such un-snug lands? Having crouched with him in the caravanserais of the East, I would like to sit beside him poking a coal fire in the waiting-room at Dover station, till a train takes us away up to London through the landscape of fields crowded in upon by fat trees, and watched over by thick-towered churches, so that I can hear his comments upon these homely scenes.

—Philip Glazebrook
Journey to Kars

Certain people are surprised that, having lived in a European country more than thirty years, I never happened to speak of it. I arrive in India, I open my eyes, and I write a book.

Those who are surprised surprise me.

How could one not write about a country that has met you with an abundance of new things and in the joy of living afresh?

And how could one write about a country where one has lived, bound down by boredom, by contradictions, by petty cares, by defeats, by the daily humdrum, and about which one has ceased to know anything?

—Henri Michaux
A Barbarian in Asia

Living overseas teaches you about yourself:

But this trip, which has scarcely begun, has already changed me; not only do I see things in clearer, truer colors, but certain aspects of my character have become magnified to an alarming degree...I detect vast capacities for impatience, resentful anger and cynicism.

—Moritz Thomsen
The Saddest Pleasure

133

For travelling, in Eothen, is as much a mental state as a physical condition. Liberated by the East from 'the stale civilisation of Europe,' Kinglake—or, rather, his first-person hero—is free to let his mind wander. With his foot in the stirrup he is in much the same reverie of free-association as a patient on an analyst's couch. For this rich young English-man, the East itself exists primarily as an exotic stage on which his own character can be more vividly illuminated than it ever was at home.

—Jonathan Raban
Introduction to Eothen

134

I felt I had done all I could with free will, and that circum-stances, the imponderables, should now take a hand. I was giving them every opportunity. I was in a city where I knew not a soul, save the few I had come to know by chance. It was a city where the mentality, the sound of the language, the hopes and possibilities, even the appearance of the people in the street, were as strange as anything I might have in-vented. My choice in coming here had been deliberate: I had a plan. My own character seemed to me ill-defined; I be-lieved that this was unfortunate and unique. I thought that if I set myself against a background into which I could not possibly merge that some outline would present itself.

—Mavis Gallant
In Transit

Whenever he was en route from one place to another, he was able to look at his life with a little more objectivity than usual. It was often on trips that he thought most clearly, and made the decisions he could not reach when he was stationary.

—Paul Bowles
The Sheltering Sky

The overseas experience adds to who you are:

I am often tired of myself and have a notion that by travel I can add to my personality and so change myself a little. I do not bring back from a journey quite the same self that I took.

—Somerset Maugham
The Gentleman in the Parlour

The proper traveler...thinks it a waste to move from his own home if nothing happens inside him as a result. I mean something fundamental, like a chemical change when two substances come into contact.

—Freya Stark
Letters

Those paper flowers, I mean, which we used to put in our finger-bowls at country dinner-tables. They look like shrivelled specks of cardboard. But in the water they begin to grow larger and to unfold themselves into unexpected patterns of flowers of all colours. That is how I feel—expanding, and taking on other tints. New problems, new influences, are at work upon me. It is as if I needed altogether fresh standards.

—Norman Douglas
South Wind

A Selected Reading List

For readers who enjoy travel narratives and expatriate fiction, we offer the following selection of classic titles.

Growing

> by Leonard Woolf
> Woolf served for two years as a colonial administrator in Sri Lanka and came home and wrote a masterpiece. A young man, just discovering himself, Woolf puzzles over the meaning of his experiences and enlightens us all in the process. The prose is as rich as the observations it records.

Jesting Pilate

> by Aldous Huxley
> If Leonard Woolf hadn't written *Growing*, Huxley would get the nod as the master of reflective travel. In format, this is the standard narrative of a journey—from India throughout much of southeast Asia and the Pacific—but little happens that doesn't start Huxley thinking. And his thoughts lift this book clean out of its genre.

The Raj Quartet

by Paul Scott

These four novels (*The Jewel in The Crown, The Towers of Silence, The Day of the Scorpion, A Division of the Spoils*) depict the British in India at the time of independence. The canvas is broad, but the theme is the meeting—and especially the clash—of two cultures. With the exception of Forster's *A Passage to India* (see below), these books come as close to being about crossing cultures as fiction can.

Journey to Kars

by Philip Glazebrook

Glazebrook, raised on stories of Victorian travelers to the Ottoman Empire, retraces their route and tries to understand the attraction. Why would these men leave the comforts of civilization at its apogee to wander the forbidding plains of Central Asia? In pursuing the answer, Glazebrook unravels the lure of abroad.

The Innocents Abroad

by Mark Twain

Much of this book is standard travelogue, but enough of it is shrewd observation (usually in the form of hilarious satire) to secure it a place on our list. Twain marvels at what he sees (he travels throughout Europe and the Mediterranean), and we marvel at the transformation of his persona from the untutored Yank into the preening pseudo-sophisticate. Skip the guidebook descriptions of Italian cathedrals and watch for Twain's skewering of human nature.

A Passage to India

by E. M. Forster

Adela Quested comes out from England to marry Ronny Heaslop and decides not to. The reason is India, or rather, how being in India changes people. In exploring this subject (the same ground he covers in *A Room with a View),* Forster gets as close as any novelist ever has to the truth of the overseas experience.

Their Heads are Green and Their Hands are Blue
by Paul Bowles
A collection of essays set in Sri Lanka and North Africa, this book confirms that Bowles is as shrewd an observer of people and mores in nonfiction as he is in his excellent novels *(Let It Come Down, The Sheltering Sky).* As with the best travel writers, Bowles' experiences prompt him into reflection; he wants to understand. And we profit from listening in.

Esmond In India
by Ruth Prawer Jhabvala
Esmond (from England) is beginning to regret his marriage to an upper-class Indian. Even more, he is bored with India. As he compares India unflatteringly with the West and as Shakuntala struggles to understand her increasingly distant husband, we watch the chasm between cultures widen.

139

Abroad
by Paul Fussell
This is a book about people who write travel books (it is subtitled *British Literary Travel between the Wars).* Fussell chronicles the careers of several of Britain's finest travel writers—Evelyn Waugh, D. H. Lawrence, Robert Byron—and examines how, through their books, England reached out to a wider world after the war to end all wars. *Abroad* is about the end of travel and the birth of tourism and how we are all poorer as a result.

The Road to Oxiana
> by Robert Byron
>
> Paul Fussell (see above selection) considers Byron the fa-
> ther of the modern travel narrative, and Fussell isn't some-
> one to dismiss lightly. *The Road to Oxiana* is a gripping, by
> turns hilarious and chilling, account of a 1920s journey to
> the Oxus. Byron is so curious, so funny, and so smart, you
> hang on every word. You can't pretend to be a serious fan of
> travel literature until you've read Byron. After you've read
> Byron, you'll search in vain for his equal. (Not that it mat-
> ters; Byron is so good that those with even half his talent
> are still remarkable.)

The Long Day Wanes
> (also known as *The Malayan Trilogy*)
> by Anthony Burgess
>
> These three novellas feature colonial expatriates in British
> Malaya before Malayan independence. The characters work
> hard to make sense out of the polyglot culture that sur-
> rounds them (part Indian, part Chinese, part Malay) and to
> understand their place—if any—therein.

Plain Tales from the Raj
> by Charles Allen
>
> Allen interviews the British who lived in—and ran—India
> prior to its independence. They describe their lives, and when
> they've finished, you know more than you might want to
> about expatriate subcultures.

The Consul's File
> by Paul Theroux
>
> An American runs a remote consulate in upcountry Malay-
> sia. He's not very busy, which leaves him ample time to get

involved in the life of the town and the affairs of the club. The consul is sufficiently jaded and sufficiently naive to make him a sharp, sympathetic observer.

The Journey's Echo
by Freya Stark
This is actually a collection of excerpts from a number of travel books by this great English traveler and travel writer. Most of her travels were in the Middle East in the first half of the twentieth century. Page for page Stark's books, and this collection in particular, contain more insight into the nature of being foreign and the meaning of the overseas experience than almost any other travel writer.

The Left Hand of Darkness
by Ursula K. Le Guin and

Out of the Silent Planet
by C. S. Lewis
The action of most science fiction novels (such as these two) is triggered by the meeting of two different cultures (or "worlds" in the parlance). Le Guin and Lewis have written some of the classics of the genre. These two examples are virtual case studies of adaptation; while each has its own engaging story line, the subtext in both cases is the importance, if not the necessity, of understanding and adapting to the ways of an alien society.

Bibliography

Adler, Nancy J. 1986. *International Dimensions of Organizational Behavior*. Boston: Wadsworth.

Allen, Charles. 1984. *Plain Tales from the Raj*. London: Futura.

Bennett, Milton J., ed. 1998. *Basic Concepts of Intercultural Communication: Selected Readings*. Yarmouth, ME: Intercultural Press.

Black, J. Stewart, Hal B. Gregersen, and Mark E. Mendenhall. 1992. *Global Assignments: Successfully Expatriating and Repatriating International Managers*. San Francisco: Jossey-Bass.

Brody, Hugh. 1975. *The People's Land*. New York: Penguin.

Burgess, Anthony. 1964. *The Long Day Wanes: A Malayan Trilogy*. New York: W. W. Norton & Company.

Carroll, Raymonde. 1990. *Cultural Misunderstandings: The French-American Experience*. Chicago: University of Chicago Press.

Crapanzano, Vincent. 1986. *Waiting: The Whites of South Africa*. New York: Vintage Books.

de Saint Exupery, Antoine. 1967. *Wind, Sand and Stars*. New York: Harcourt, Brace & World.

Durrell, Lawrence. 1957. *Bitter Lemons*. New York: E. P. Dutton.

Eliot, T. S. 1962. "Four Quartets." *The Complete Poems and Plays, 1909–1950*. New York: Harcourt, Brace and World.

Fleming, Peter. 1985. *Brazilian Adventure*. Excerpted in *A Taste for Travel,* edited by John Julius Norwich. London: Macmillan.

Fussell, Paul, ed. 1987. *The Norton Book of Travel*. New York: W. W. Norton.

Gannon, Martin J. and Associates. 1994. *Understanding Global Cultures: Metaphorical Journeys Through 17 Countries*. Thousand Oaks, CA: Sage.

Gibbs, Paul. 1992. *Doing Business in the European Community*. London: Kogan/Page.

Glazebrook, Philip. 1984. *Journey to Kars*. New York: Penguin.

Grove, Cornelius. 1990. *Orientation Handbook for Youth Exchange Programs*. Yarmouth, ME: Intercultural Press.

Hall, Edward T. 1990. *The Silent Language*. New York: Anchor Press/Doubleday.

Hall, Edward T. 1984. *The Dance of Life*. New York: Anchor Press/Doubleday.

Hall, Edward T., and Mildred Reed Hall. 1990. *Understanding Cultural Differences*. Yarmouth, ME: Intercultural Press.

Harris, Philip R., and Robert T. Moran. 1987. *Managing Cultural Differences*. Houston: Gulf Publishing.

Harrison, Lawrence E., and Samuel P. Huntington, eds. 2000. *Culture Matters: How Values Shape Human Progress*. New York: Basic Books.

Hickson, David J., ed. 1997. *Exploring Management Across the World*. London: Penguin Books.

Hickson, David J., and Derek S. Pugh. 1995. *Management Worldwide: The Impact of Societal Culture on Organizations around the Globe*. London: Penguin.

Huxley, Aldous. 1985. *Jesting Pilate*. London: Triad/Paladin.

Jhabvala, Ruth Prawer. 1987. *Out of India*. New York: Simon & Schuster.

Kingsley, Mary. 1984. *West African Studies*. Excerpted in *The Englishman Abroad*, compiled by Hugh and Pauline Massingham. Gloucester, UK: Alan Sutton.

Kohls, L. Robert. 2001. *Survival Kit for Overseas Living: For Americans Planning to Live and Work Abroad*. 4th ed. Yarmouth, ME: Nicholas Brealey/Intercultural Press.

Lawrence, D. H. 1984. *Letters*. Excerpted in *The Englishman Abroad*, compiled by Hugh and Pauline Massingham. Gloucester, UK: Alan Sutton.

Lawrence, T. E. 1939. *The Seven Pillars of Wisdom*. London: The Reprint Society.

Le Guin, Ursula K. 1977. *The Left Hand of Darkness*. New York: Ace Books.

Lewis, C. S. 1965. *Out of the Silent Planet*. New York: Macmillan.

Mantel, Hilary. 1987. "Last Morning in Al Hamra." *Spectator*, 24 January.

Marquardt, Michael J., and Dean W. Engel. 1993. *Global Human Resource Development*. Englewood Cliffs, NJ: Prentice Hall.

Massingham, Hugh, and Pauline Massingham. Compilers. 1984. *The Englishman Abroad*. Gloucester, UK: Alan Sutton.

Mernissi, Fatima. 1975. *Beyond the Veil: Male-Female Dynamics in a Modern Muslim Society*. Cambridge, MA: Schenken Publishing.

Mole, John. 1995. *Mind Your Manners: Managing Business Cultures in Europe*. London: Nicholas Brealey.

Moorhouse, Geoffrey. 1984. *India Britannica*. London: Paladin.

Oberg, Kalvero. 1981. "Culture Shock and the Problem of Adjusting to New Cultural Environments." As quoted in Pierre Casse, *Training for the Cross-Cultural Mind*. Washington, DC: SIETAR.

Osland, Joyce Sautters. 1995. *The Adventure of Working Abroad: Hero Tales from the Global Frontier*. San Francisco: Jossey-Bass.

Scott, Paul. 1979. *The Jewel in the Crown*. New York: Avon.

Shames, Germaine W. 1997. *Transcultural Odysseys: The Evolving Global Consciousness*. Yarmouth, ME: Intercultural Press.

Shepard, Steven. 1998. *Managing Cross-Cultural Transition: A Handbook for Corporations, Employees, and Their Families*. Bayside, NY: Aletheia Publications.

Stark, Freya. 1988. *The Journey's Echo*. New York: The Echo Press.

Stewart, Edward C. 1972. *American Cultural Patterns: A Cross-Cultural Perspective*. Yarmouth, ME: Intercultural Press.

Stewart, Edward C. and Milton J. Bennett. 1991. *American Cultural Patterns: A Cross-Cultural Perspective*. 2d ed. Yarmouth, ME: Intercultural Press.

Storti, Craig. 1997. *A Few Minor Adjustments*. Washington, DC: Peace Corps.

Taylor, Edmond. 1964. *Richer by Asia*. New York: Time/Life.

Thomsen, Moritz. 1989a. *Living Poor: An American's Encounter with Ecuador*. London: Eland.

———. 1989b. *The Saddest Pleasure*. Saint Paul, MN: Graywolf Press.

Trompenaars, Fons. 1994. *Riding the Waves of Culture: Understanding Diversity in Global Business*. New York: Irwin.

Washington Post. 1986. 27 November.

Windham International. 1999. "Global Relocation Trends 1999 Survey Report." New York: Windham International.

Index

(including all authors quoted)

For those who have enjoyed *The Art of Crossing Cultures*, Intercultural Press and Nicholas Brealey Publishing provide here the introduction to Craig Storti's companion volume, *The Art of Coming Home*.

THE ART OF
COMING
HOME

CRAIG STORTI

Introduction

*When I go back I know I shall be out of it; we fellows who've
spent our lives out here always are.*

—*Somerset Maugham*
The Gentleman in the Parlour

It is a well-known fact that living and working overseas take some
getting used to. Cultural adjustment is a much-studied and increasingly well-understood phenomenon. Books have been written about it and people regularly attend workshops and seminars
to learn how to cope with it. In a sure sign the phenomenon has
arrived, the phrase "culture shock" has been plucked from its ori-
gins in the intercultural field and is now commonly used by the
man in the street to describe adjusting to any difficult or unexpected set of circumstances.

With the front end of the overseas experience so well discussed
and documented, it's surprising to find that the back end, coming
home, has received relatively little attention. After all, most of
the people who go overseas eventually come back. Yet, few books
on readjustment are available, and training seminars on the subject are still very much the exception rather than the rule—even

among those same companies and organizations that spend good money preparing people to go overseas.

None of this would make any difference, of course, if reentry were as simple as most people expect—merely a matter of picking up where you left off. But all the evidence, both anecdotal and statistical, confirms that it is in fact a complicated and usually difficult experience. Indeed, most expatriates find readjusting back home, now commonly known as reverse culture shock, more difficult than adjusting overseas ever was. Consider:

- In one study of American returnees, 64 percent reported "significant culture shock" upon repatriation.
- In another survey, 64 percent of Dutch and 80 percent of Japanese expats said they found coming home more difficult than adjusting overseas.
- Only 7 percent of returning teenagers said they felt at home with their peers in the United States.
- More than 50 percent of Swedish exchange students said they "didn't fit in" when they returned to Sweden.
- Seventy-five percent of returning soldiers in one study said they found reentry "difficult, time-consuming, and acrimonious."
- More than 50 percent of the executives in a survey of U.S. corporations said they experienced social reentry problems upon repatriation.

When you think of the number of people temporarily living and working overseas at any one time—such as expatriate business people and their families, government and military personnel and their families, exchange and study-abroad students—nearly all of whom are eventual returnees, the case for helping people understand and deal with readjustment becomes even stronger. Using the United States as an example, at any given time nearly 2.5 million Americans are in residence overseas (excluding permanent residents of foreign countries), at least a quarter of whom are likely to return home each year. Other countries may have even higher numbers (or at least a higher percentage of their overall population).

The reentry arithmetic becomes even more compelling when you consider that readjustment has been found to have a profound impact not only on the returnee but also on family members, colleagues, and close friends. When you add all of the figures together, the worldwide number of people significantly affected at any one time by the phenomenon of reentry must be in the millions.

And all indications are that the number of would-be returnees is growing, especially in the private sector, as globalization becomes a fact of business life. Over one hundred thousand U.S. companies now do business internationally, for example, and more than twenty-five thousand of these companies operate offices abroad. Patric Oster has observed in his article, "The fast track leads overseas," in *Business Week* magazine,

> Globalization means more managers must make stops abroad. General Motors Corp. has 485 U.S. managers overseas, up 15 percent from 1991. Gerber Products Co. is thinking of tripling [its] number. Likewise, Motorola Inc. [has] expanded its rank of senior executives overseas by 10 percent and plans another 10 percent increase. "We expect it to continue to increase as a reflection of the fact that markets are opening up overseas," says a Motorola spokesman. (1993, 64)

The case for paying attention to readjustment is supported by yet another set of numbers: the financial costs. It has been estimated that it costs the average company roughly the equivalent $250,000 U.S. a year in salary, benefits, and subsidies to keep an expatriate and his or her family in an overseas assignment. With an average overseas stay of three to four years, the investment in the employee adds up to nearly a million dollars.

That's all right, of course, as long as the employee stays with the company and the investment is recouped, but the statistics here are also not very encouraging.

- Twenty-five percent of returnees leave their parent company within one year of coming home.
- Twenty-six percent of returnees were actively looking for another job.
- Forty-five percent of companies surveyed reported "problems with attrition" among returnees.
- Seventy-four percent of returnees did not expect to be working for the same company one year later.
- Two-thirds of returning professionals complained of suffering from the "out of sight, out of mind" syndrome upon reentry.

Employees leave their organizations for many reasons, of course, and people who don't go abroad also move on, but the most common reason for returnee attrition is dissatisfaction with the position the employee is assigned upon reentry. It's interesting to note in this context that while two-thirds to three-quarters of companies in the United States offer some kind of orientation for employees heading abroad, only 28 percent have a repatriation program for returnees. This seems backwards, for surely the greater risk to the organization is not the expat who doesn't work out overseas—and is normally reabsorbed into the company back home—but the successful expat who comes home only to become the frustrated returnee who then leaves the company altogether. The fact that approximately "one in four returning expatriates leave their firm...represents a substantial financial and human capital loss," Stewart Black and Hal Gregersen have observed,

> *especially if the skills, knowledge, and experience that the individual gains are important to the firm and scarce in the internal or external labor markets. Thus, the practical reasons for investigating the repatriation adjustment process*

seem as compelling as those for understanding expatriate cross-cultural adjustment. (1991, 672)

Behind all these numbers are people, of course, many of whom are wondering what's happening to them. Let's listen in for a moment.

> *It was very nice to come back and see the people and get settled.... But all of a sudden, I went from this position of being a manager [overseas] and having virtually complete control over what I did and what the people did who worked for me to being just one of the people here again—having a director sitting twenty feet away and two managers sitting even closer to me. I was answerable to all three, after having no boss at all.*
>
> —American businessman

> *My job description did not even exist when I came home. I felt as though I had no status in the company. In fact, everybody was asking, "Hey, what are you doing here."*
>
> —Finnish expatriate executive

> *When I got back, I found I was no longer a round peg in a round hole, but a square peg trying to find a hole that didn't seem to be there at all.*
>
> —New Zealand aid worker

> *When I got back to my hometown in Ohio and went to work, I fell back into hanging out evenings in the neighborhood tavern with my old buddies. After about two weeks of that I gave up the tavern. They didn't care about the problems of the Indians in Peru, and I didn't give a damn what happened to the Indians in Cleveland.*
>
> —American Peace Corps volunteer

People pushed and shoved you in New York subways or they treated you as if you simply didn't exist. I hated everyone and everything I saw here and had to tell myself over and over again, Whoa, this is your country, it is what you are part of.

—American college student

Coming back home was more difficult than going abroad because you expect changes when going overseas. It was real culture shock during repatriation. I was an alien in my home country. Old friends had moved, had children, or just vanished. Others were interested in our experiences, but only sort of. They simply couldn't understand.

—Finnish expatriate spouse

Everyone seemed unfriendly and snobbish. It was impossible to break into the right cliques and make friends. Clothes mattered more than personality, and competition was tremendous. The activities through which I was expecting to meet people weren't as easy to get involved in as I'd thought they would be. People did seem to go to parties every weekend, just like in the movies, but I was never invited. I knew no one and it was fairly obvious they did not want to know me.

—American teenager

I knew what I had to do. I didn't say the ice cream was awful, even though I said it to myself. I said to my friends, "Quito is wonderful." They [invite] me to go to parties, but I am not enthusiastic.

—Ecuadorian exchange student

We came from a lovely rural area of England to the Los Angeles area. We were in an apartment and knew no one. Our son's bike was stolen and we had roaches. I reacted the same way I did when I arrived in Korea: I didn't go out and I wouldn't let the boys out. I felt threatened.
> —American military spouse

My advice about coming home? Don't.
> —Japanese businessman

In this book we will consider the key issues of the phenomenon of reentry and offer suggestions—for returnees, their family and friends, and employers—for dealing successfully with this experience. Chapter 1 examines what we might call generic reentry, the most common issues returnees face regardless of what they were doing overseas, their role in the family, or what they will be doing upon their return. Chapter 2 explores the stages of reentry and describes how returnees can expect to feel as they pick their way through this transition. Chapter 3 looks at the return to the workplace, the issues employees face upon reentering their organization after an overseas sojourn. Chapter 4 considers the return of spouses, young children, and teenagers—issues specific to these three groups (and not treated in chapter 1). And chapter 5 examines four special populations: exchange students, international foreign aid volunteers, military personnel and their families, and missionaries and missionary children.

We realize, of course, that there are as many experiences of reentry as there are people coming home, that every returnee could write his or her own book and no two of those volumes would be alike. There is reentry after a year overseas, after two, after four. There is reentry from a country you loved and hate to leave, and from a country you did not enjoy and are happy to turn your back on. There is reentry from a country radically different from your own and from a country quite similar to home, from developed countries and from developing countries. There is voluntary and involuntary reentry, expected and totally unexpected reentry, premature and delayed reentry. There is reentering at age thirty, with children, and at age fifty-five, as grandparents. There is your first reentry, your second, and your fourth. You may return to the same house you left and the same job, or you may return to a different part of your home country and to a different job. Or to no job at all. There is the reentry of people who were running away from home and of expatriates who went abroad kicking and screaming. And there are cultural differences, too; the reentry of a Japanese family to Japan won't be the same as the reentry of a German family to Germany or an American family to the United States.

Reentry, in short, is a deeply personal experience and a cultural one as well. While we have tried to select and discuss the most common concerns of most returnees in most countries, no single returnee will have exactly the experience we describe in these pages, and some will have experiences that are not mentioned here. Even so, we expect most returnees will recognize themselves repeatedly in this volume.

While returnees themselves will be the most avid readers here, loved ones, friends, employers, and colleagues of returnees will likewise find a great deal to ponder in these pages. To the extent that their lives are affected by what returnees go through during reentry, family, friends, and others can only be helped by having their own understanding of the experience. To the extent they may want to help returnees through the experience—or at least not make it harder for them—such understanding becomes essential. "I [had] two trips and two experiences [when I went] abroad," one returnee noted. "The [overseas] trip influenced me. The [return] influenced everyone around me."

We close with a caveat: Readers of this book could be forgiven for concluding that an overseas experience doesn't stack up very well against the apparent heartache of reentry, that unless one's sojourn abroad is extraordinarily rich, it could never compensate for the problems of coming home. But this is not at all the message here. Reentry, for all its minor and a few major annoyances, can't begin to diminish the lustre of an expatriate experience. Indeed, it is in some ways precisely because the overseas experience is so rich and stimulating that reentry becomes a problem. In other words if you are having trouble readjusting, it's probably because you had such a terrific time abroad.

Moreover, simply because reentry can be frustrating, lonely, and generally unpleasant at times is not to say that it is a harmful experience or a negative one. After all, frustration, loneliness, and unpleasantness are very often the precursors of insight and personal growth. Maybe reentry doesn't always feel good, but then feeling good isn't much of a standard for measuring experience.

Make no mistake about it; reentry *is* an experience to be reckoned with, but when the reckoning is done and the accounts are cleared, you are likely to find that the price you paid for your overseas sojourn was the bargain of a lifetime.